THE QUEST FOR COMMON VALUES

Report of a Seminar
Organised by The Inter Faith Network for the UK
10 December 1996

0154348

This book is due for return on or before the last date shown below.

21. JUN 99

CANCELLED 14 MAY 2002

CANCELLED
27 MAR 2003
OCT 2003

1 8 JAN 2005

1 3 APR 2005

0 8 MAR 2007

3 0 JUN 2008

Don Gresswell Ltd., London, N.21   Cat. No. 1208

DG 02242/71

0951743279

The Inter Faith Network for the UK

The Inter Faith Network was founded in 1987. It works alongside its member organisations to increase mutual understanding and respect between the faith communities of the world religions represented in the UK today. It also works more widely within society to promote an appreciation of the importance of religious identity and inter faith understanding. To carry out these aims, the Network:

- **Links 80 member organisations** including: representative bodies from Britain's nine major faith communities; national inter faith organisations; local inter faith groups; academic institutions and bodies concerned with multi faith education
- **Acts as a central information and contact point** for people wanting information or advice on inter faith affairs, or faith community contacts
- **Provides a national forum** for multi faith discussion of key issues
- **Fosters local inter faith initiatives** and organises meetings around Britain to bring together those working on inter faith issues
- **Publishes materials** to assist inter faith work around Britain
- **Organises seminars and working groups** on specific topics, such as religious identity and the law.

Further information from The Inter Faith Network: 5/7 Tavistock Place, London WC1H 9SN (tel 0171 388 0008; fax 0171 387 7968).

Contents

Preface by

Brian Pearce,
Director, The Inter Faith Network for the UK

This is a report on a consultative seminar convened under the auspices of The Inter Faith Network for the UK and held on 10 December 1996 at Barnard's Inn Hall in London by kind permission of Gresham College. It contains the texts of the presentations by the five main speakers, Chief Rabbi Dr Jonathan Sacks, Dr Nicholas Tate, Ms Monica Taylor, Professor Bhikhu Parekh and Bishop Gavin Reid, together with a summary record of the intervening periods for questions and the closing general discussion.

Introduction

For some time the Network has had a focus on the issue of values in a multi faith society and it has developed useful links with a wide range of those working in this field. The purpose of this seminar was to bring together a number of those involved in current and prospective values initiatives in order to explore the relationship between these, to take stock of recent developments and to exchange experience and ideas for future work in this field.

The Network is grateful to all who took part in the seminar and in particular to those who provided the five stimulating introductory presentations. The seminar was limited to a small number of participants in order to encourage informal discussion during the day alongside the more formal presentations. A full list of the participants is at Annex B to this report.

The seminar was primarily intended as a forum for discussion and was not expected to reach a tidy set of agreed conclusions. In this preface I offer some personal reflections on the topic in the light of the day's debate and in the process focus on some of its main themes.

Our Sources of Inspiration and Authority

The varying contributions to the seminar discussion underlined that we look to different sources for our "values" and that in doing so we acknowledge different authorities for them. Those who belong to a particular religious community will look to its scriptures and to its traditions as these have been developed and interpreted over the centuries. At the same time, there are many in our society who look to philosophies which do not derive, directly at least, from a religious tradition. All of us draw on the historical experience of our different communities, the accumulated wisdom of our cultures and on our own personal experience and reflection.

Two Possible Approaches to Seeking Common Values
In his presentation Professor Bhikhu Parekh pointed to two different approaches which can be adopted in framing a set of common values. The first is to formulate an abstract set of values, grounded in some concept of a universal morality constructed from first principles, which is claimed to be "true for all". This approach can carry with it the implication that authority can and should be vested in that abstract set of values and that the teaching of different religious and cultural traditions are in some way secondary in character, although they may embody these abstract values to some degree. This approach will be resisted by many people and particularly by those who see the authority of their own tradition grounded in some transcendent reality. It can also lead to an intolerance of those who are not ready to subscribe to the supposedly "universal" set of values in preference to those of their own tradition or culture. Some recent attempts at the creation of a "universal ethic" have been criticised on the grounds that in practice they owe too much to a post-Enlightenment Western liberalism.

An alternative, and more pragmatic, approach does not challenge the primary authority accorded by believers in them to the world's different traditions and philosophies. Instead it is based on an exploration of whether there is in practice an overlap in the values upheld by these different traditions and which can therefore be seen to be shared by them. It is this second approach which is the more promising one.

The Nature of Consensus
Any attempt to formulate a set of shared values on this more pragmatic basis cannot appeal for its acceptance *either* to some notional "universal ethic" *or* to the authority on which the values of one particular tradition are based. If, however, a patient exploration of the overlap between the values which each tradition upholds does turn out to reveal common moral ground between them, then the very fact of this consensus provides its own functional authority for them within the wider society to which the members of these different traditions belong. But because it rests on the extent to which values are "shared" by different traditions it does not undercut the authority of those traditions for believers in them.

2

A consensus on fundamental matters of this kind is unlikely to be universal. But clearly it needs to be very broadly based if it is indeed to posses this functional authority within a society and to command the commitment which it needs to evoke. Furthermore, if it is to be genuine then we must not be tempted to facilitate it through excluding dissenting voices from the debate. It was stressed both by Professor Parekh and Dr Nicholas Tate that it is important not to absolutise this pragmatic social consensus as constituting "the truth" *per se*. There is always likely to remain some tension between the content of this consensus and the convictions held within different communities within society because it will not manage to incorporate all aspects of any individual tradition.

This was apparent in the dissatisfaction expressed by some critics at the outcome of the School Curriculum and Assessment Authority (SCAA) National Forum on Values in Education and the Community on the grounds that this did not adequately reflect *their* values because it did not go beyond the limits of the consensus which could in practice be established among the Forum's participants. There are, as Monica Taylor pointed out, inevitably difficult issues of process and representation involved in initiatives of this kind. But there was a general welcome at the seminar for the initiative which SCAA has taken and a recognition of its importance.

Concern is often expressed that the authority of traditional sources of moral values has been eroded within our society. It is sometimes suggested that the development within Britain of a more diverse and plural society has in itself contributed to fragmentation and incoherence in the moral sphere. Others have suggested that the greater diversity within our own society derives less from the recent migration here of people from other cultural backgrounds (who in any case form only a small percentage of the total population) than from the fragmentation of the indigenous culture itself under the impact of secularisation and technological change. Some, however, have questioned whether there ever was a past time of stable "common moral ground" in our society and are in consequence sceptical about the whole "common values" enterprise.

If a genuine and widely based consensus on moral values is to be formed within present day British society then there will certainly be a need to explore not only the overlap between the resources of our different *religious* traditions but also the overlap with the moral values of those who are not committed to any particular religious tradition but nonetheless have moral values which they strongly uphold. The process of secularisation has been an important factor in shaping our society. But a deeper understanding is needed of the character and effects of this process. It is particularly important to distinguish between, on the one hand, a dogmatic materialist reductionism, which refuses to recognise any spiritual dimension to human life, and, on the other, the more open attitude of those who acknowledge the reality of the moral and spiritual realm, but are unable or unwilling to express their spirituality through involvement in the life of a religious community or through the conceptual framework and vocabulary of a religious tradition. One of the issues which was raised in the seminar was whether we can find a vocabulary for our spirituality which can be shared by both those who base their values on the existence of God and those who do not. The presence among the world's religious traditions of non-theistic Buddhism and Jainism may perhaps provide a bridge of understanding here.

The Concept of "Core Values" and the Complexity of Applying Them

The evidence of recent attempts to draw up sets of common values suggests that substantial agreement can in practice be reached on a set of "core" values, such as honesty, compassion and respect for life. The Global Ethic promulgated at the World Parliament of Religions in 1993 and the set of values listed by the SCAA Forum have both won substantial endorsement.

The importance of being able to reach agreement on "core" values should not be underestimated, since if there really are no common or shared values within a society then there can be no possibility of a shared public discourse between its members and no possibility of a plural civic society, or indeed of affirming in any meaningful sense that we share a common humanity. The identification of a set of shared values can provide us with reassurance that we can indeed have a shared society and a shared future together. Even though shared values may at one level be grounded in a pragmatic consensus, at a deeper level they are rooted in our personal and community convictions and commitments. The discovery that they are shared with those who follow other faiths or philosophical traditions can be a source of encouragement and lead to a mutual reinforcement of these convictions.

At the same time, it can be more difficult to reach agreement on how to apply in practice these shared "core" values to specific problems and particular situations, especially as different values often appear to pull us in different directions. So it is important not to exaggerate the degree of agreement on common moral ground. We live in a complex world and in applying basic "core" values to

4

complex situations there will be disagreement even between those who belong to the same religious tradition or philosophical background. As was pointed out in the seminar discussion, the interpretation and application of values need to take account of different circumstances and of differences in time and place.

We need a debate on values which is both intelligent and intelligible. It is not easy to offer the straightforward moral leadership for which many look. In a "soundbite" culture public debate is often impatient with qualified and balanced statements and prefers crude assertions and slogans which cannot match the complexity of real situations as they arise in actual life today.

Diversity and Dialogue

The development of our more diverse society in itself invites a debate on the extent to which we can find common moral ground. As was pointed out by Professor Parekh, the concept of "common values" can be used either to subvert, or to undergird, the notion of a plural society. Those who belong to the dominant cultural tradition may assert, without any real debate, that their own values are the "common values" of the society as a whole and other cultural traditions may then be seen as threats to the maintenance of these "common values". Or "common values" can emerge from a process of debate which takes account of the perspectives of different groups within the society. so that these values are seen to be *genuinely* held in common.

As was argued in the seminar, it is likely that in any society there will be a predominant tradition which shapes the values of a majority of that society's members. But that does not affect the desirability of seeking a wider consensus through participative dialogue. Nor is the value of the dialogue process simply a pragmatic one. Within the Jain tradition there is the concept of *anekantavada*: the belief that no one perspective on an issue contains the whole truth. This points to the need to value the perspectives and experience of others so that diversity is not simply respected but is seen as being in itself a valuable resource for a society. This does not require us to embrace the much feared moral *relativism* and abandon concepts of right and wrong. A recognition of the *relativity* of our own position does not require us to accept the philosophical attitude expressed in relativism that there is no room for the concept of the absolute, whether in terms of a deity, or of absolute goodness or absolute truth. It means simply that we recognise that as finite human beings we can have only a *relative* grasp of the absolute.

To engage in the process of dialogue and seeking consensus therefore does not mean that in consequence we have to surrender our own beliefs and values. Each of us holds our own beliefs and values to be true (if not proven) as otherwise we would abandon them. But while retaining them we can still acknowledge the benefit which is to be gained from the process of debate with others and the value of the different contributions we can all make to this in the light of our different experience of the common reality we all inhabit.

So the contribution of all to the debate on values is not only to be welcomed on grounds of social justice and participation but also as a potential source of enrichment and enlightenment for ourselves. The circle of this debate needs to be an inclusive one because we all have something to contribute to it. We also need a dialogue which does not remain at the level of a distant politeness but engages in discussion in depth of the values which our traditions and philosophies have to offer in addressing particular sets of ethical issues, as we seek to identify areas of agreement on these and to understand better the reasons for disagreement.

Turning Abstract Values into Virtuous Lives

During the seminar some concern was expressed that an abstract debate on values can be a sterile process. This is certainly the case if the fruits of the debate are not carried over into the lives we lead. There was widespread agreement that it is important not simply to identify values which we hold in common but also to find ways in which we can "energise" not merely the pursuit of the good, but the "love of the good". Here the distinction drawn between "values" and "virtues" is a useful one: values need to be put into effect in living virtuous lives.

In this context there was a natural focus in the discussion on the role of values in the education of children, with whom the future of our society rests. Chief Rabbi Dr Jonathan Sacks and others stressed the crucial roles of home, school and community and the need for these three contexts to be in alignment in promoting a coherent framework for the moral development of children and young people. But it was recognised that moral values cannot satisfactorily be taught as abstract entities. They need to be lived out to provide examples which young people will want to follow. The ethos of a school needs to be exemplified in the life of the school community and it will be of no use for adults to exhort children and young people to lead moral lives if they fail to live exemplary lives themselves. "Do as I say and not as I do" is never a very effective piece of advice!

The Public and the Private Realms
The suggestion is sometimes made that it is possible to distinguish between our private behaviour and personal relationships on the one hand and on the other our public conduct in the wider society in which we live. This may hold true to some extent and there has been a nervousness about the intrusion of the state into matters of "private" morality. But the seminar discussion recognised that the private and the public inevitably interact and that there does need to be a moral coherence between our private and public values.

There was some discussion about the distinction between the basic requirements of civic society and the more specifically political process, including the role of the state. There are widely different views about the extent and character of the role which government and our other public institutions should play within society. But there would be general agreement that the political process must never be regarded as a "value free zone": morality is concerned with the whole of human life. As has been said, all political issues are moral ones even if not all moral issues are political ones. Moreover, many would argue that public policy and action programmes have a significant impact on the kind of lives which people can in practice lead and on whether particular values are encouraged or discouraged within society. Values are clearly central not only to the personal but also to the social and civic dimensions of our lives.

A Shared Ethic for Our Journey Together
There are those who believe passionately in the desirability of a plural society and hold this to be the ideal. Others may see pluralism as a passing phenomenon and hope that the time will come when everyone follows their particular religious tradition and adopts its beliefs. But, regardless of which of these positions they hold, most people will recognise that in the present time we need to find ways in which we can live equitably and fruitfully together as fellow citizens within our shared society, drawing on the common values we do have.

We need to transcend a narrow individualism to forge a binding and mutual commitment to seek the common good. We need to have a "shared ethic" for our encounter and for our journey together which leads us to behave in ways which create the trust and security which will enable us to be honest and open with another. A deep

7

and trusting dialogue is required if we are to overcome the barriers of misunderstanding which history has built. If, in this process, we are to benefit from the understanding and experience which others can bring to our common life together, then we all need to practice humility and self criticism.

The Inter Faith Network for the UK has as its central purpose the building of good relations between people of different faiths and beliefs and the promoting of mutual understanding between them. Those of us involved in its work believe that a willing acceptance of the need to come together in mutual respect and openness is in itself a crucial "value" and its practice in our personal lives and the lives of our communities a crucial "virtue". It is part of our mutual obligation to respect and value one another as fellow human beings. Through affirming with commitment and conviction the values which we share with others we can help to nurture these values more effectively within our society and in the process provide it with surer moral foundations.

Conclusion

There has always been a debate about morality and there no doubt always will be. Bishop Gavin Reid referred to the suggestions which have been made by the Churches for a nationwide debate on values linked to the Millennium and involving in it everyone, of different faiths and of none. We hope that the Network's recent seminar will prove to have been a useful contribution to the development of that debate and a better understanding of the concepts with which it will need to deal.

Opening of the Seminar

The members of the seminar were welcomed to Barnard's Inn Hall by *Dr Andreas Prindl*, President of Gresham College. He explained that the College was founded in 1597 by Sir Thomas Gresham when it had seven professors, one to teach on each day of the week, and lectures were given at 12 noon in Latin and at 1.00pm in English. Today, Gresham College offers a wide range of public lectures and organises seminars on a variety of topics. It has a concern itself for issues of values and it was therefore most appropriate for the College to host the seminar.

Mr Om Parkash Sharma, President of the National Council of Hindu Temples and Co-Chair of The Inter Faith Network, thanked Dr Prindl for his words of welcome and expressed gratitude to Gresham College for its willingness to allow its facilities to be used for the seminar. He explained that his Co-Chair, the Rt Revd Roy Williamson, Anglican Bishop of Southwark, was due to have chaired the day's proceedings but was unable to do so because of illness. Mr Sharma had asked the Network's Director, Mr Brian Pearce, who had been responsible for making arrangements for the day's seminar to steer the day's proceedings after the first keynote address. Mr Sharma went on to set the scene for the seminar.

Mr Sharma: As you know, the title of our seminar is "The Quest for Common Values". Some horrifying incidents have taken place in our society in recent years, such as the murder of little Jamie Bulger and the stabbing of the London headmaster, Philip Lawrence. These have led to good deal of soul searching about the moral state of our society. There have been suggestions that we have lost our way in moral terms as a society. There have also been suggestions that because we are now a more plural and religiously diverse society this may have led to a greater degree of fragmentation. Many people are asking whether there is indeed a set of common values which we share and which can underpin our society. These are some of the issues we intend to tackle today.

To open our proceedings, I have the very greatest pleasure in introducing our keynote speaker who has been at the forefront of the recent debate on values in the Britain of today. He is Chief Rabbi

Dr Jonathan Sacks. His books and articles and radio talks on this topic will be known to many of us. We are delighted to have this opportunity to welcome him for the first time to a meeting under the auspices of The Inter Faith Network and we look forward with great interest to what he has to say to us.

Presentation by

Rabbi Dr Jonathan Sacks

Chief Rabbi of the United Hebrew Congregations of the Commonwealth

It is a great privilege to join you this morning and to share in your and our quest for common values. It is an even greater privilege for a speaker to be allowed to be totally superfluous! Your other speakers today, all of them combined represent a formidable array of expertise. It is tremendous to have with us Dr Nicholas Tate of SCAA, who has done so much to advance this particular project and this general debate; Monica Taylor, the Chair of the Values Education Council, which will take this debate forward in the years to come; Professor Bhikhu Parekh, who has written so brilliantly about this subject; Bishop Gavin Reid, who, together with his working group on the Millennium, has done so much to ensure that this will hopefully be more than a giant ferris wheel on the South Bank and will be an event of real moral and spiritual depth. Since they will say everything that needs to be said, I intend to step back from the contemporary debate and to look at the issues of today from a very distant historical perspective. From there we can perhaps see a little more clearly than we can from close to.

Today we are in the middle of a Jewish festival, the festival of Chanukah, which is known as the Festival of Lights, during which on each day for eight days we light the candelabra in our homes to remind us of the candelabrum that once burned in the Temple Jerusalem, each night adding an extra candle. I want, if I may, to tell the story of Chanukah as a story of a search for common values. In fact, I am going to tell the story of the story of Chanukah.

What, at the simplest, most external level, is the story of Chanukah? During the reign of Alexander the Great, Greek influence spread as his conquest cut through great swathes of Africa and Asia. One of the areas that came under Greek rule was Israel, first under the branch of the Ptolemies which was based in Egypt and then under the Seleucids based in Syria. So Jews for the first time came face to face with Greek culture. Many Jews welcomed this; after all, Greek culture was dazzling in terms of its military prowess, its art and architecture, its drama and its philosophy and some Jews were fascinated and intrigued and became more Greek than the Greeks. Others, of course, resisted, seeing it as all together too physical, too material, too pagan a culture for Jewish tradition. Those were the tensions in the air for a century.

However, it came to a point in the year 167 BCE when a Seleucid ruler, Antiochus IV, decided forcibly to impose cultural assimilation on the Jews of Israel. A statue to Zeus was erected in the Temple and Jerusalem was turned into a Greek polis. A series of decrees were issued that in effect forbad Jews to practice their religion. That resulted in a rebellion centred around some religious Jews, around the family of the High Priest Mattathias the Hasmonean and one of his sons in particular, Judas Maccabeus, who organised resistance to Greek rule. At first, there were only a handful of guerilla fighters. The early rebels were nearly all killed. One reason was that their leaders were religious and could not fight a battle on the Sabbath and therefore when there was a battle on a Sabbath they were completely wiped out. Then, after three years of fighting, a relatively small group of people won one of the great victories of all time against the Seleucid army and re-conquered Jerusalem and re-dedicated the Temple. That is why we celebrate Chanukah, or more precisely, that is why *they* celebrated Chanukah, which means rededication.

That is the story of Chanukah as it is told in the histories of the time by the ancient Greeks and by Jewish historians in the First Book of Maccabees. It is still, to some extent, the story that we tell.

However, this is only the "outer" story. Because if that were to be the totality of Chanukah we would not be celebrating it today and for the last 1900 years. Why so? Because 230 years later, around the years of 66-72 CE, a new opposing force appeared in the Middle East and in Israel specifically, namely the Romans. Again, there was a Jewish rebellion. This time it was a disaster. The result was that Jerusalem was reconquered by the Romans, the Second Temple was destroyed, and all vestiges of Jewish sovereignty were lost. Everything that had been regained was now lost and we know from the evidence of the ancient Rabbinic literature that in many parts of Israel the festival of Chanukah was not observed because there was nothing now left to celebrate. So, as the Talmud records, there was a proposal to abolish Chanukah.

So, how is it that Chanukah is evidently not abolished after all and that we still celebrate it? It was at that stage that a very different story which had been recorded in the literature suddenly became significant. It was a little story, recorded in probably the first document of Rabbinic Judaism, the scroll called Megillat Ta'anit, the scroll of Fast Days and Festivals, which told the following story. When the victorious Maccabee rebels entered the Temple which they had conquered, they found in it one cruse of oil which had not been defiled by pagan rites and with this they were able to re-light the sacred candelabrum in Jerusalem, the menorah, and, by a miracle, the light, which should have burned for one day, instead lasted for eight days. That is the story recorded in Megillat Ta'anit and, of course, it became a great symbol of the eternal renewal of the Jewish spirit or, should we say, in that phrase which became the subtitle of Jewish history, in the words of the Prophet Zechariah: Jewish people survive "not by might, nor by power, but by my Spirit, says the Lords of Hosts." Because that symbol and that story remained, and because it was re-enacted in Jewish family homes in the form of lighting the candelabrum, that is why Chanukah survived. The story of the great military victory is not its point, but the story of the oil in the lamp that survived.

Now I want to ask a very simple question: How is it that Jews were telling two different stories about the same event? It is, of course, a common saying that when in other cultures people have conversations, Jews have arguments!

There was a fundamental division in the Jewish people in the early centuries. According to the historian Josephus, the Jewish people were divided into three groups. There were Essenes, Sadducees and Pharisees. Essenes belonged to a group of apocalyptic sects and were expecting the Millennium and the imminent overthrow of civilisation. Who were the Sadducees? They were the governing elite and also provided the Temple priesthood. They were guilty in the eyes of many Jews of the cardinal sin in Judaism of combining kingship and priesthood, politics and religion, which in Jewish tradition have always been kept apart. The Sadducees were a religious group but we can call them the party of the state, of the central institutions of the government and the Temple in Jerusalem. Who were the Pharisees? Or, more precisely, to get away from that word which has bad connotations, who were the Rabbis? Rabbis saw the centre of Jewish life, not in government or the Temple, but rather in three things: the home, as the centre of religious ritual; the synagogue, as the centre of community; and the school, as a centre of continuity for the transmission of the community's values from one generation to the next.

What was the difference between the Sadducees and the Pharisees? Put in simple terms, the Sadducees were interested in the state, the Pharisees of Rabbinic Judaism were interested in society, in the non-political aspects of the way we live together. Today, we would say they were interested in community. That is how two different stories emerged. On the one hand we have the story of the state, about the military victory of the Hasmoneans who recovered

Jewish sovereignty and rebuilt the Jewish state and on the other we have a more modest story about lighting candles.

How was it that the Sadducees, who were at the time the most powerful group, the ruling class, lost the argument? What happened to that little group of religious individuals, who used to gather in small rooms together and who were without much political influence? What led them to emerge so rapidly as the most powerful force in Jewish life, indeed the dominant force for the next 2,000 years. This is the real story. Here we come to the crux. Chanukah began with a war for the survival of Jewish identity in the face of the surrounding Hellenistic culture. Initially, the first military victory led Jews to think that is how you win: you fight a battle and you defeat your enemies. That is how you win the battle for your identity. However, over time they realised that the real battle for identity is not fought in the arena of war, but it is fought and won by sustaining a way of life and its values over time. That is the only way to win the battle and, in that way, the fortresses are the schools, the heroes are the teachers and the weapons are not swords but books.

By the middle of the first century CE, already before the destruction of the Second Temple, the Rabbis had organised an entire national, universal and compulsory system of education: a massive network of schools sustained through communal funds, from age 6 to age 17, the first, I believe, of its kind anywhere. They thus laid the groundwork for the survival of Judaism across the world until today. In the battle for the survival of their identity and their way of life, the Ministry of Defence was transformed into the Ministry of Education. That was the crucial development. The Second Temple was destroyed in the year 70 CE. A hundred years later there were no more Essenes and there were no more Sadducees. All that were left were Pharisees, the Rabbis, because they had foreseen the nature of the battle and had prepared for it and they dominated the Jewish world during the centuries that followed.

That is why Judaism survived. Instead of a people which owed its identity to being a nation with an army it became a people which owed its identity and its survival to three things: the strength of the home, the strength of the synagogue and the strength of the Jewish school. That is the story of the story of Chanukah. That is how, over the course of two centuries, one story was succeeded by another. It is how Jews moved from being a group of people predicated on a state to a group of people who owed their survival to a society.

It seems to me that this is not unlike what is happening to us now. Because we have been faced with a series of formidable problems: family breakdown, rising crime, self-reinforcing cycles of poverty, the rise in depressive illness among adults and among children and so on. We have begun to recognise that the most serious issues we face are social problems. And what do I mean by social? I mean they are problems that cannot be solved by us acting alone as individuals. They are problems that can only be partially solved by the State acting on our behalf. These are problems that can only be solved by society, by all of us acting together. That is a very profound shift in the terms of the contemporary debate. You have seen that shift in a whole range of thinkers in this country from all across the political spectrum, as unlike one another as Professor A.H. Halsey, Roger Scruton, David Selborne, John Gray, and we have a very distinguished representative of this school in our midst today, Melanie Philips, who has taken this argument forward so much in her book and in her journalism, and many others. It is what is called on the right of politics "civic conservatism" and what is called on the middle and left of politics "communitarianism". It is no coincidence that there have suddenly emerged into the forefront of public debate the three issues that emerged 2,000 years ago when Judaism faced a crisis in its continuity: the three issues of family, community and schools, together with that framework of values that knits all three into an interlocking and mutually supportive relationship. That is what happens when we realise that the problems we face are problems of society rather than of the state. Every culture faces these problems if it is to survive and everything comes back to those three institutions and the set of values that relate to them. I told the Chanukah story because it is the same crisis in which we Jews found ourselves a little over 2,000 years ago.

What I think is so valuable about the SCAA report on the teaching of values in schools is precisely that it begins with this understanding. It asks the right questions. It asks about the ways in which schools might be supported in teaching values and it asks what might be the values that schools should teach, or to quote the report, "to promote, on society's behalf". Dr Tate and SCAA's National Forum saw from the very beginning that schools cannot do it alone. They have to do it in conjunction with families and communities, all three working together within a shared framework of values. There is no other way of doing it. Schools are not independent variables; they cannot function alone; they certainly cannot succeed alone.

The question is, can it be done in a society as diverse as ours? I think it can, for an obvious reason. People make a massive mistake when they confuse our religious, our ethnic and our cultural diversity with *moral* diversity. I think those are quite different things. It is surely the case that we tell different stories and we celebrate different rituals. We sing different songs. We give different reasons for what we do. However, any enduring faith or culture will find a central place for those three values of the family, the community and the school and for linking them together because this is the only way that a civilisation can persist across time. It has been my experience in working with other faith communities that despite profound differences in narrative, ritual and culture, we share a striking similarity in our commitment to those institutions and values. What is more, one of the most helpful features of British society over the last three or four years, has been that at moments of crisis when a call goes out, as it did after the killing of Jamie Bulger, after the murder of Philip Lawrence and after Frances Lawrence's marvellously moving call to our society, there has been a very profound sense that a national chord has been sounded, a collective mood expressed. I believe there is far greater consensus than we allow to be imagined and that it is there ready to be articulated: not in great detail but in broad outline.

We have to guard against the establishment of this consensus being politicised, particularly in the period leading up to a general election. We have to develop, and insist on, a rather longer attention span than the modern sound bite, when it is decided to reduce the length of "Thought for Day" from three minutes to 2 minutes 45 seconds on the grounds that this is the length of the listeners' attention span! We have at least to make the case that it may conceivably take more than 2 minutes and 45 seconds to articulate the moral problems of our society! Whenever people discuss morality in public life they quote Macaulay's famous essay on Byron from 1843 where he says that nothing is so ridiculous as the British public in one of its periodic fits of morality. Macaulay is supposed to be saying that we should not moralise in public, but, of course, Macaulay never said that and never believed that. He was one of the great Victorian moralists. To what did he object? He objected to the culture of the soundbite or what he called "periodic fits". He was *not* against discussing morality in public, but against discussing it for 5 seconds and then forgetting it for five years until the next scandal or the next crisis. That is what he meant. In other words, if we are to sustain a debate, it must be sustained at a level of seriousness in our collective discourse which lifts it from the merely trivial.

I can say against anyone who is pessimistic about the possibility of changing the climate of opinion: Do not be. Because, speaking from personal experience, when I first raised these questions about the family, community, culture and the transmission of tradition six years ago in my Reith Lectures, I felt myself to be a very lonely voice indeed. Today, only six years later, I feel myself to be part of a collective mood in which many voices are taking part. That is in only six years. It took 200 years for Jews to make the cultural shift from Chanukah as a military story about victory to Chanukah as a moral and spiritual story about lighting candles. That did not happen without intense argument and division, but in the end it did. So it will be, I believe, that our own society will make that same transition from state to society and to the institutions which sustain society which are inherently *moral* institutions. It will, and it must, because at the end of the day we are social animals and that, by definition, means moral animals. Therefore we will always seek to rebuild the institutions that sustain and animate our moral and social life.

*   *   *

Questions and discussion following Dr Sacks' Presentation

Ms Humera Khan: In this seminar we are talking as members of a number of different religious traditions. Taking on board other people's particular histories can be problematic for us. I empathise with your desire to distinguish in terms of Jewish history the political and social spheres and to focus on the social one, but is not part of our problem in Britain today a political one? You have emphasised the role of the family. But unless there is support at the political level for families, for dealing with their health and education needs and alleviating these and other pressures on the family, particularly in minority communities, surely it is going to be difficult to develop the kind of society we want?

Chief Rabbi Dr Jonathan Sacks: There are perhaps two issues here. Can we pursue values, which both you and I will want to set within a religious framework, in a culture and society where people come from different religious backgrounds and many people have no religious framework for their lives at all? I believe that we can, because there are certain central values that are shared in any civilisation which persists over time. Firstly, there is a set of moral

17

rules, for example, "Do unto others as you would have them do unto you", "Love your neighbour". They are all summarised by C.S. Lewis at the end of his book "The Abolition of Man" where he lists the basic set of moral rules which all cultures share.

Secondly, there is a set of moral *virtues*. There are lots of different games such as soccer, rugby and cricket. But what is in common between them is that anyone who is to play any kind of game needs to have certain skills and certain training. He has to exercise, to be fit, to have good brain-body coordination, and has to be capable of working in a team and so on. If we apply this to the moral life, even though we envisage families differently, you will need a set of virtues such as honesty, integrity, trustworthiness and persistence: the entire catalogue of virtues that the SCAA report has listed. Since Aristotle these virtues have been identified and many of them have remained stable throughout time. So again, we agree on moral virtues.

Thirdly, and very importantly, there is another set of virtues that exist in a society where people are different from one another. These have been called the "liberal virtues" and without all of us displaying these virtues we are not going to get along at all: these are respect for differences; the ability to listen; the ability to present a reasoned case; a respect for impartial procedures; and a willingness to compromise in the public, if not in the private, domain. These liberal virtues are essential to any society that is not a homogenous one. So there are three elements which we will all hold in common whatever our tradition may be and I think that we can identify very important areas of agreement on these matters even if our religious histories are different ones.

Ms Humera Khan: I question whether it is possible to create a "universal" set of "values and morals" which reflect the diversity in our community. Inevitably in trying to set a "universal perspective" we will have to compromise on "language" and even "perspective" in order to "fit in" with it. Therefore, it is inevitable that the criteria of the majority culture for the values and norms of society will be the dominant ones. This is not necessarily negative as long as we are upfront about it. In this context, I have an expectation that Christianity will take the lead. Is it not inevitable in any society that the majority perspective dominates and that its language, perspective and norms will influence how other religions, cultures and perspectives "fit in" to any supposedly "universal" set of values and norms?

Chief Rabbi Dr Jonathan Sacks: Everyone comes from a particular cultural perspective. The Jewish community represents only a half a percent of the population of this country. Traditionally Jews have not taken their beliefs into the public domain. Today, quite deliberately, I told a Jewish story to a non-Jewish audience. We have to learn that each of us *can* tell our story and that we can tell it to people who do not come from where we come from. That takes a lot of courage and a lot of care because we tend to be very embarrassed about sharing our stories, which are very precious to us, with people who do not hold them sacred and when we tell our story we have to tell it in terms that other people understand. In the Hindu, Jewish, Muslim, Sikh and other communities we have to recognise that we are part of a larger community called "society" and that we need to engage in a public conversation within that society. We have to be ready to broadcast and to use public debate. If we want other people to respect the fact that we are different, we in turn have to respect the fact that those other people are different. It takes a long time to get to this stage but we are getting there and that is one of the great strengths of this country. We have to get there because otherwise you will find that the stronger our individual identities are the more conflicting and ghettoised our society becomes. So the short answer is that we have to talk together. But you know that already!

Dr Nicholas Tate
Chief Executive, School Curriculum and Assessment Authority

Thank you for inviting me to speak at this seminar. As the head of an organisation, the School Curriculum and Assessment Authority (SCAA), which has tried to do its bit to further your own aim of promoting "mutual respect and understanding between the different faith communities in this country", through our work on religious education, I am delighted to take part in this discussion of common values. It is a topic on which my organisation has done a great deal of work over the last year and it is also a topic close to my heart.

This seminar comes at a crucial time for this work. The consultation on the recommendations of our National Forum on Values in Education and the Community has just come to an end. We are collating responses to the consultation exercise in preparation for a further meeting of the Forum in January after which we will be submitting advice on ways forward both to my Authority and to the Secretary of State for Education and Employment.*

I cannot share with you the findings of the consultation exercise in advance of finalising the analysis and submitting it first to the Forum. But I should like to take the opportunity of clarifying what we have been trying to achieve and putting right a few misconceptions.

As part of the consultation, groups of parents were asked to comment on each of the Forum's proposed statements of value. Although these parents were generally supportive of the statements, according to the report on the consultation which I have just been given, they viewed with scepticism the idea of a "shared moral code" asking — (and I quote from the report) "Whose moral code would this be?"

This is a very revealing question. Their assumption, it seems, is that different groups, or perhaps different people, have different moral codes, that there are no beliefs about morality that are shared by all of us. Why else would they ask "whose moral code" are we going to ask schools to promote?

It was precisely this mindset that prompted our initiative in the first place. It is not only parents who think that the differences

---

Note The National Forum's Statement on Values is at Annex A to this report.

between us prohibit agreement on morality. It is also, unsurprisingly perhaps, young people. My colleague, Marianne Talbot, who is working with SCAA on this exercise and teaches philosophy at Brasenose College, Oxford, tells me that her first year philosophy undergraduates come up to Oxford believing that morality is a matter of personal taste and that, therefore, one cannot properly argue about moral matters. One also finds frequently among trainee teachers the fear that if they impose moral values upon their pupils they will somehow be violating the autonomy of these young people who ought to be free to choose their own moral code.

The sources of these attitudes lie partly in the complexity and diversity of our society; partly in the decline of organised religion; partly in Marxism, with its notion that ideas and values are instruments of oppression; partly in the pervasive post-modernism which threatens to replace truth with the idea that everything is discourse, fiction or construct. I would love to explore further the origins of these attitudes. However, I do not propose to do so, both because of lack of time and because my views on these matters were quite cleverly parodied in The Times Educational Supplement last week. It was an accurate, and not entirely unsympathetic, parody. It had me referring to the Chief Rabbi, which I frequently do, as I have been much influenced by his writings and because he is so very quotable.

Suffice it to say that we set out to challenge these attitudes and to show that whatever our differences our common humanity enables us to achieve consensus on much of what we value, and this in turn ensures that we can co-operate in the search for moral truth. Last January we started the exercise by holding a conference on moral and spiritual education at which delegates agreed that it was important to try and identify these values. To do this, many felt, would be to recover a language of morality, lost to many people through the decline of organised religion, and to help us reaffirm our membership of a community defined by certain shared beliefs. The latter is crucial. All or most previous societies and cultures have had a shared story to tell themselves about who they were, where they came from and where they were going.

This country, which for most of its history has been a fairly monolithically Christian country, had such a shared story once. It was based on the narratives of the Bible. One hears it loud and clear in the literature of the Middle Ages. One hears it still in Tudor and Stuart times: in the sonnets and sermons of Donne, and (loud and clear still) in the poems of Milton. People continued to hear it throughout the eighteenth and nineteenth centuries, in the Book of Common Prayer and the Authorised Version of the Bible, but weakening now and competing with contrary voices. Then, finally, in our century, the story peters out. It has now almost ceased to be heard within the wider society (and our educational system has some responsibility for that) and even, at times, within the Church.

Clearly, what we now have are a number of different stories, co-existing within a society which is religiously more plural than it ever was. It is a reflection of that society that we are all gathered here today. What we also now have, and this is what is unique about modern society, is a majority who do not appear to share any of these traditional stories and who, moreover, have been unable to replace them with any kind of new story based on a post-religious view of the world. Richard Dawkins may be doing his best, but I don't sense that his particular Darwinian view — and Darwin undoubtedly tells a story — is widely shared even among the many people in our society who lack religious beliefs. And even where it is shared people lack a shared sense of its implications for their lives.

All this makes the task of education and of organisations like SCAA very difficult indeed. It is not surprising that those involved in education feel that the issues are too big for them to resolve or that they have come to feel that certain things are best not even talked about. Nor is it surprising that people tried to discourage me from embarking on our current SCAA initiative on the grounds that it would be too difficult and controversial. It is also not surprising that people turn with relief to the kind of relativist and post-modernist views I have been describing. How much easier if all values, and even knowledge, were simply matters of choice and if education were seen as preparation for a solipsistic world in which each individual constructs himself, makes his own fictions, creates his own universe, without any other foundation than that these fictions please him or her or are useful to him or her. Such a response to a world in a state of flux is hardly surprising. But it is not a sustainable basis either for society or for an education system.

Our initiative through the Values Forum was designed to provide an alternative response to flux and pluralism based on a reaffirmation of those things we have in common. It was an attempt to fill a vacuum for those who had a vacuum to be filled. It was an attempt to reinstate a story that everyone could tell and that everyone could share, even though clearly for some people it was only the basis for other and more compelling stories that they also continue to tell within their particular traditions. Put like that our initiative was an ambitious one. That explains why it has attracted so much attention, both positive and negative. We have been delighted by the support we received in the Forum from members of many different faiths and by the public statement of support for our initiative issued by the Council of Christians and Jews and endorsed by the Archbishop of Canterbury, Cardinal Hume, the Chief Rabbi, Archbishop Gregorios of Thyateira and Great Britain, the Moderator of the Free Church Federal Council, and the Moderator of the General Assembly of the Church of Scotland.

But we knew we would be attacked as well, both for the idea and the content of the proposals. The most recent assault, admittedly in my opinion a lightweight one, came yesterday with the publication of a pamphlet by Dr John Marenbon of Trinity College, Cambridge by the think tank Politeia. Because this is fresh in my mind and because it perpetuates some of the misconceptions about the exercise which have plagued us all along I will refer to it at a number of points during the final part of my talk. Let me list some of these misconceptions.

First, some critics (in this case not Dr Marenbon) fail to distinguish between what the moral consensus of our society actually is and what we might wish it to be. We have always been clear that the Forum's task was to establish the extent to which, within itself, there was a consensus and that SCAA would then see to what extent this consensus was shared by the wider society. It would have been quite inappropriate to have asked the Forum to evaluate the various moral codes that different people would like to persuade society to adopt and then decide which one it preferred. The Forum therefore cannot be criticised for failing to insist, for example, that valuing human life means opposing abortion or that a family unit based on a couple who have been through a wedding ceremony is superior to one based on a couple who have not. There is *not* a consensus within our society about these matters, even if there is a majority view. To recognise that this is so is not to make a moral judgement, either way, on these issues. Nor is it to adopt the relativist position that these are simply matters of opinion or taste. It is just to recognise a fact.

The second misconception, linked to the first, is that the Forum's statement of values was intended to replace other moral codes and provide the blueprint for a new moral order. Again the problem comes from assuming that 'what is' — the actual consensus — is "what ought to be". But no one ever made that equation. The purpose of the exercise was to re-establish the notion that there was a moral consensus, to identify what it consisted of, and to use it as a basis for a renewed moral consciousness within society. Critics of the statement the Forum has formulated do not appear to disagree with what is in it, just to demand that it be added to and made more precise.

These demands also reveal another misunderstanding: that the statement is designed to be the sole basis of moral instruction in schools. This is perhaps not surprising given that it went out for consultation under the aegis of SCAA However, we have always been clear that its purpose, as far as schools are concerned, is to identify the consensus about values that society is authorising schools to pass on to the next generation on its behalf. We have not suggested that schools have to adopt it in this form, or that it be added to the National Curriculum, or that it be taught didactically.

Nor have we suggested that the values outlined in the statement are exhaustive. Clearly any statement of values that are common to us all will leave out values that are very important to certain groups or indeed to a majority of people within a society. Many schools, for example, require children to be presented with opportunities and experiences through which they see a stable, loving and lifelong marriage as a normal and desirable feature of life. Nothing we have said conflicts with this. A Government that is keen to encourage such relationships, as the best basis for bringing up children and of minimising social problems (and these are matters which are legitimate concerns of Government), might even wish to encourage this.

Our intention, however, has been to provide schools with a structure for developing their own statements of values, following discussions with parents, teachers, governors and students. It was always envisaged that schools would wish to turn the Forum's statements of shared values and principles for action into more precise rules, for example into "do's" and "don'ts" that habituate students into the right sort of behaviour.

I fully agree that schools need to have codes of behaviour about cheating, stealing, bullying, courtesy, litter, respect for property and all these very important things that are vital for young people's moral development. But these are things best dealt with at school level, not through national prescription. Almost all schools have lists of rules: Indeed our recent survey showed that only 8% do not. Many have agreed statements of values. But many — 36% according to our recent survey — do not. The aim of the exercise was to support schools in their delivery of a moral and spiritual education: to give teachers confidence in the knowledge that the values they promote are *ours* and not simply *theirs*.

Finally, the idea that we were somehow trying to impose a moral code on the nation rather than just proclaiming (and celebrating) the existence of a consensus has led some of our critics to suggest, rather uncharitably, that we have been less than honest in our efforts to gauge people's views. Dr Marenbon for example, suggests in his pamphlet that we set up a conference with "carefully chosen delegates" and published a report of its deliberations "presented so as to justify a particular course of action". Similarly, one of the members of a small dissenting minority on the Forum, who were keen that we presented as a consensus something that I am afraid was clearly not part of a consensus, has implied in an article in The Times that we have somehow slanted the consultation on the Forum's statement to exclude the views of parents and of the general public.

Nothing could be further from the truth. The consultation has consisted of a MORI poll of a representative sample of adults, questionnaires to a structured sample of 3,000 schools and 700 organisations on our general mailing list, structured face to face meetings with groups of parents, teachers and school governors, and an analysis of unsolicited responses, and there have been many from members of the public. In response to enquiries, these members of the public were sent our consultation document, but not a questionnaire, both because it would have been inappropriate to have mixed up a representative sample with a self-selected one and because of the impossibility of constructing a questionnaire capable of dealing with the miscellany of issues one normally finds in responses by the general public to a wide-ranging set of issues. But we are recording and analysing all such there responses and will report them accurately to my Authority and to Ministers.

The whole storm in a teacup about the consultation is in itself a reflection, I fear, of the moral climate in which we operate. There is still such a climate of cynicism and distrust that far too many people assume the worst of those with whom they disagree. By demonising their opponents, they excuse their own sometimes unethical behaviour. But theirs is a naive cynicism, attributing motives which are quite impossible and for which there is no evidence, and imagining conspiracies that bear no relation to the muddled way in which busy public bodies normally go about their business. It would be good if one effect of establishing shared values were to show people the common impulses that can lie behind disparate actions and to make people more inclined to give others the benefit of the doubt, at least in the first instance. We lack sufficient charity in public debate.

In conclusion, there are two alternatives to the search for common values. Neither in my view is an acceptable response to the problems of the kind of society in which we live. The first is to abandon the search and to promote, in particular through the state school system, a set of values which those in authority feel ought to be promoted but which are not generally shared within society. This was the line taken by a very small number of members of the SCAA Forum who, for example, wished us to use the statement of agreed values to insist on chastity before marriage. One may sympathise with the wish to re-state a position that has been an important part of the Christian tradition, and indeed of other traditions. One may also agree that it is important that young people learn that this has been, and still, is a strongly held view for many people. But it is clearly not the case that there is a consensus on such a position within our society. To try to base one's shared values on such a premise runs the risk of reinforcing people's assumption that there are no such things as shared values.

The second alternative is to accept that there are no common values worth speaking of and to leave everyone, including children, to work out (or not) their own values. Some will be Roman Catholics; some will be Muslims; some will be postmodernists; some will be followers of New Age cults; some will find meaning in following the dictates of whatever latest fashion our consumerist society throws at them. And no one will have anything in common. Schools will likewise be free to take whatever moral line, or none, they and their parents wish. This appears to be the brave new libertarian world of Dr Marenbon's pamphlet, and it is a frightening one. It is frightening both because of its casual dismissal of the idea of a wider community, which though plural, is based on shared values and because of its failure to recognise the extent to which we live in a society in which many people are being brought up outside traditional belief systems.

Therefore, I see no alternative to the search for, and promotion of, common values as the basis of a society in which people feel they belong and in which they have duties towards each other. You are an inter-faith network and I can see the problems that face you in searching for values shared by people of all faiths and none. Inevitably you want to go further. However, establishing the values we all share will, in my view, encourage people to think once again about the source of all values and maybe therefore to renew their acquaintance with God. That is an additional reason to work together, alongside men and women of good will of no faith, on the task which our Forum was set and which, as I understand it, you have set yourselves in this seminar.

* * *

Questions and discussion following Dr Tate's Presentation

Mrs Rosalind Preston: How have teachers responded to the current SCAA exercise on values? It may look as if we in society are yet again asking teachers to take on fresh and difficult burdens.

Dr Nicholas Tate: It was only yesterday that I received the preliminary analysis of our consultation process. But judging from the reports of the discussion groups which have met, the response of teachers seems to have been generally supportive and the messages which have been coming back are about wanting help in implementing this approach. I do think that there is in general an acceptance that it is the responsibility of schools to promote the development of young people. The Chief Rabbi pointed to the crucial role of schools as instruments in this work. But I think that schools do feel that they have not always been supported by the rest of society in what they are trying to do. A key part of our consultation has been to seek views on how this support could best be provided. There has been a variety of suggestions on this, including the provision of model syllabuses (along the lines of the RE syllabuses produced recently), the production of resource material and case studies.

I do not sense that schools are seeking to evade their responsibility in this field but schools do get uneasy when it appears to be suggested that they have the *sole* responsibility for the moral development of young people. Clearly the primary responsibility for this rests with the family and in the home, but the home and the school need to work together very closely. Sadly, for many of our children, the one stable institution in their life is the school which they attend. In their case the school has a particularly vital role to play. One of the depressing aspects of the Politeia pamphlet was its suggestion that moral purpose was irrelevant to education. But thinkers about education, from Aristotle onwards, have seen the moral development of young people as being at the very heart of education.

Dr N J Prinja: I am not sure how far the Hindu point of view has been taken into account in the work of the SCAA Forum. Hindus do agree with the need to establish and promote a set of common values, but our concern is over how the teaching in schools of these

27

values is to be monitored. For example, in a discussion about how to teach about human rights in Manchester schools, Muslim representatives proposed that the focus should be on Bosnia and Kashmir. In the case of one syllabus, of only one page in length, two lines were spent talking about the struggle to have a Sikh homeland of Khalistan. People who come from those areas of the world will recognise that these are political issues. Is there not a serious risk that particular political agendas will be promoted under the guise of teaching about human rights?

Dr Nicholas Tate: There were Hindu representatives in the Forum alongside those of other faiths and we have been very keen to involve the Hindu community in our work. You are pointing to the danger that individual teachers, and those who devise syllabuses and set examination questions, may treat issues in a biased way, without necessarily being aware that they are doing so. It is generally recognised that it is important to be impartial in dealing with these matters. One of the recent Education Acts introduced a specific legal duty on schools to deal with political issues in an impartial way because of instances in the early 1980s of material of a blatantly partisan kind being used in the classroom. So there is now a legal as well as a moral duty on schools to avoid this kind of unfortunate behaviour.

The best way of tackling this concern is through making schools and their teachers more conscious of the underlying purpose of addressing issues of this kind within the curriculum. That is one reason why I would like to see model syllabuses and case studies and to include in the National Curriculum, when we come to revise it in due course, some explicit recognition of the responsibility which all schools have for promoting moral education. This would make it easier to issue authoritative guidance for schools. There is already a statutory obligation, if in quite broad terms, for schools to promote the moral development of young people and the way that schools respond to that obligation is one of the matters looked at by OFSTED in its inspections. I am sure that their inspectors are alert to the risk of partisan treatment of sensitive topics. In terms of syllabuses and of examinations, it is my Authority's responsibility to monitor this and we do so. But we look to community representatives to draw our attention to situations in which it is believed that this impartiality has been broken.

Dr Helen Haste: I found the SCAA document to be really quite good. But I have some worries. Firstly, it is very difficult to teach human rights without becoming involved in political issues. Surely we have to recognise that it is not possible to separate the political from the moral, but that we need rather to find an acceptable way to deal with this overlap?

Secondly, I am worried about the risk of confusing consensus with truth. It is a good post-modernist position to say that consensus may give good guidance on how we should live our lives. But while we can arrive at a consensus on values and go forward on that basis, we should not call this "truth". The danger is that this would suggest that it derives from some kind of inspiration or external authority of a kind which not all of us would acknowledge.

Thirdly, we live in a plural society and we have to find a way of respecting the diversity of backgrounds within it. This is a conference under inter faith auspices. In passing you mentioned those who have no religious faith. I would in general terms share the world view of Professor Richard Dawkins. We have to recognise that many people are not followers of a particular faith and are therefore not part of a community of faith. So we cannot assume that everyone has a faith community to which they can return as a source of authority and inspiration for their lives and from which they can derive their values. In our public education system we have to find a way in which we can inspire young children to lead moral lives without suggesting that this means that they must come back to God in order to do so. It would not be appropriate for state schools to say so. We have to find a way that does not claim that moral values necessarily have to be derived solely from the synagogue, the church, the mosque or the temple, while at the same time respecting the position of faith communities.

Dr Nicholas Tate: I was not suggesting that schools should tell young people to return to God but I would say that one of the consequences of pointing to a moral consensus would be that young people would begin to think about the sources of moral truth. They might indeed decide that the sources of this were other than God or might decide that the source was God. But it would not be appropriate to promote a particular faith stance in school.

On the point about consensus and truth, I would say that one does not necessarily have to be a person of faith to believe that there is moral truth. Many people, including moral philosophers, would accept the notion of moral truth even if they would not necessarily ground this in a deity. So I think it is right to talk in such terms. Having established a factual consensus, which is all that I can claim has been done, one can view that consensus in different ways. Some might see it simply as a consensus and nothing more; and see behind it a whole set of different stories. However, I would regard the kind of values which are shared within our society by people of all faiths and none (and indeed, as the Chief Rabbi said, which have been shared by previous cultures and civilisations), as having their basis in moral truth. No doubt many of us here would do so. But that does not mean that the role of SCAA is to commend these values as "the truth".

Mr Huddleston: You rejected a didactic method of teaching values. So what do you have in mind in terms of the content of model syllabuses for moral education?

Dr Nicholas Tate: I am very clear that moral education in schools consists of a number of different elements. Most importantly, it consists of the ethos and atmosphere of a school and that involves a whole variety of contributory factors and in particular depends on the vision and leadership of the headteacher. I would like to be commending to schools suggestions about good practice in that area.

Secondly, there is a moral dimension to the wider curriculum. Again, in drawing attention to this, we have been misunderstood as trying, for example, to insert artificially a "moral" unit into an A-level maths syllabus, although there are indeed moral aspects to the teaching of mathematics.

Thirdly, I do think that the explicit discussion of moral issues as part of an organised programme should be taken up by schools alongside the preparation of students for citizenship and telling people about the structures of the society in which they are living. I would like to see a variety of different programmes or syllabuses for schools that embrace the sort of matters which I have talked about and which are currently taught under the heading of PSE (Personal and Social Education). Our concern there is that this tends to focus on problems, crises and difficulties to do with health issues, AIDS, and sexual morality rather than dealing with moral issues as ones which arise across the whole of life. That is why a specific focus on values in education would be valuable.

Ms Monica J. Taylor
Chair, Values Education Council

As Chair of the Values Education Council (VEC), I welcome the initiative of the Inter Faith Network, in orchestrating this seminar, which is very much in the spirit of VEC, to facilitate and promote discussion about values issues. I am both honoured and appreciative of the invitation to speak in such illustrious company.

I want to speak from both personal and professional perspectives. Personally, I shall speak from a rather more secular position than the majority of you here would espouse, but one which is not unsympathetic to religion. I also note that I am the only female speaker — not an unusual position — and what I have to say may also be seen as coming from a female perspective. Professionally, I shall speak as an educationalist and on behalf of the membership of VEC. In its own way, VEC aims to bring together those with religious commitment and those without in an ongoing debate about values in education.

Currently, VEC has over 30 individual members and 30 or so organisational members — including associations and university departments concerned with, for example, citizenship, technology, religious education, philosophy and sex education. Some of these organisations themselves have a large membership; one has over 2,000 members. Many representatives of these organisations worked together for over three years before we established the VEC in 1995. Its common focus is values. We see it as a bridge between different interest groups which also share an interest in values as one of their primary aims and purposes.

VEC is concerned with both values education and values in education — thus with the way in which society and education interconnect. The purpose of the Values Education Council — whose wording we weighed at some length — is "to promote and develop values education and values in education and to help individuals develop as responsible and caring persons and live as participating members of a pluralist society".

The aims of VEC are to promote dialogue, provide a network, work together with those responsible for public policy and support those engaged in values education. At the moment VEC does not have prepared position statements. It is more concerned with taking seriously — valuing — the *process* of valuing — arriving at agreed views, than advocating particular substantive values as such.

In this light I should like to comment on the title of this seminar — both in terms of the 'quest' and 'common values'. In so doing, I hope to relate the contribution which the VEC and its member bodies can make to current deliberations, such as that initiated by SCAA with its National Forum on Values in Education and the Community, about which Nick Tate spoke. I also want to speak a little about a subject on which I imagine Bikhu Parekh will have more to say, namely, what the quest for common values means in a culturally diverse, pluralist society. For it is awareness of contemporary diversity in all its forms — social, economic, religious, cultural, and so on — which gives rise to debate about the nature of society and the kind of society in which we wish to live, which is, in turn, implied in the quest for common values. Embedded in what I say will be some values not commonly found in the more positive, content-oriented lists.

I should also like to emphasise the extent to which it seems to me the values debate — especially the moral values debate, which I assume we are focusing on here — brings together the personal, the professional and the political. I do not believe these debates are divorced from political realities. I know from two international conferences this year — *the Journal of Moral Education's* 25th anniversary conference (Morals for the Millennium), which had participants from 33 countries and every continent, and the more recent Association for Moral Education conference in Canada (Developing Personal and Social Responsibility: Practitioner and Researcher in Common Cause) that moral values concerns are shared globally. Indeed, in our own continent other European countries are demonstrating more continuing interest, involvement and commitment to values in education.

The implementation of two of VEC's aims — promoting dialogue and influencing public policy — can be illustrated in relation to the SCAA Values Forum. I should say that I personally, but not as Chair of VEC, was a member of the Forum. VEC has responded to the SCAA consultation after consulting with as many member organisations as was possible in the limited time available. VEC member organisations are among the leading organisations concerned with values in education. Several such organisations and a few teacher unions sent me copies of their own responses. Their comments relate to the search for values in education and the community, not just as a matter of producing a list of values, but as to the process of discussion and dialogue.

I, personally, and the VEC, applaud the initiative of SCAA and the risk taken by Nick Tate in entering the murky waters of values.

I was glad to hear, just now, that he has no regrets. Whilst acknowledging the difficulty of the task, nevertheless, it is a revealing comment on values in education that we have had to wait eight years for explicit attention to be given to values since the Education Reform Act enjoined upon schools a 'balanced and broadly based curriculum which promotes the spiritual, moral, cultural, mental and physical development of pupils at the school and of society'. The core curriculum of the National Curriculum has had absolute priority. Yet the values domain, and especially that of the life of the school, is the context into which the National Curriculum falls. Moreover, values penetrate all teaching and learning in the curriculum.

The Forum looked not just at the work of schools but also at society, work and the family. One of its outcomes is a statement of values and related principles for action, endorsed by members of the Forum. I think it would be surprising if these 'values' — self, relationships, society, possibly less so the environment — were not endorsed in the wider consultation. However, I also question whether they are what we usually mean by 'values'. Rather, they appear like "values domains" in which values issues, conflicts and choices occur. It seems to me that the Forum's statement may be seen as passing itself off as substantive content when it is rather bland and vacuous to the point that it rather resembles form only. By this I mean that the statement is clearly only a framework of values which schools, and perhaps other institutions, need to reinterpret and specify as guidance and rules appropriate to their own contexts. This, in turn, will suggest criteria for monitoring and evaluation.

I was interested in Nick Tate's remarks about the misleading media publicity surrounding the Forum's statement, some of which suggested publication of a list of values, such as honesty, taking personal responsibility for one's actions, or respecting the rights and property of others (which incidentally were recommended to schools in the discussion document on *Spiritual and Moral Development*, reissued by SCAA, in 1995). Indeed, the Research group of the Forum, of which I was a member, was particularly anxious not to produce such a list because of its superficiality. But a fixation at this level is indicative of the type of media reportage.

What has happened — the values publicity in the media — falls, of course, into a political context and a desire to reassert authority of various kinds. To be anecdotal: at a recent meeting of a trust interested in promoting Christianity in education and society, in the context of the current media concern with values, two MPs advocated a return to the Ten Commandments. Yet I believe evangelical and other Christian colleagues present were also concerned about that statement relating to education in a maintained school context in a culturally plural society. So I want to alert us to the fact that, because it is by definition controversial, the moral values domain comes with political tags and hence with personal predilections. We have only to consider how the recent media values debate moved swiftly from Mrs Lawrence's article in *The Times*, to the banning of guns and knives and, with the intervention of the Secretary of State for Education, to reintroducing corporal punishment.

There are limitations to the value of lists of values. In view of the concern which was expressed about relativism in the initial SCAA conference, Education for Adult Life (held in 1996), particularly based on reports of university students' views, it is interesting to note that ten years ago a study by Don Locke was reported (in the *Journal of Moral Education*, 15,2, 150-6) of philosophy students trying to decide on a contemporary decalogue. Difficulty was experienced with producing positive formulations of principles not admitting of exceptions, which also had only general and obscure implications for actual conduct. Locke suggests it might be more constructive to devise rules which could be formulated more precisely, as guidelines, but which could admit of exceptions. We might consider how this relates to SCAA's principles for action.

I want to say something about the consultation aspect of the Forum, which I see as being a particularly important part of pluralism and the quest for common values. The comments I have seen and heard about the Forum have raised a number of questions about:

- The selection of individuals and whether they were 'representing' the organisation, with which they were listed as affiliated; if so, what did 'representation' mean?
- How the groups worked; the influence of group on group; whether the groups were working to a prior agenda.
- The simplistic questions in the consultation documents; the short-scale timing of the consultation (a common feature of such initiatives), which did not allow other organisations to properly consult with their members; the rushed and superficial nature of the survey process which will result in a speedy, generalised overview which will be represented by the media as a consensus. But what does consensus mean?
- The 'principles for action' which apparently offer simple solutions to complex realities and which may seem patronising

34

to teachers who see their task as riddled with ambiguities. SCAA's 'principles for action', like OFSTED inspection criteria, are, in turn, dependent on articulation, perception, and interpretation in local contexts.

Some comments about the potential clash between consensus and conviction. In the context of The Inter Faith Network, conviction will usually be associated with strongly held beliefs about particular matters of substantive content or values. Sometimes there has to be a compromise of conviction about specifics in order to achieve consensus about general principles. But conviction is the more important and more difficult with respect to process; disposition, will and commitment are significant here, too. Seeing that the climate for dialogue is appropriate, that rules which are inclusive in terms of participation are taken seriously, that there is a sincere attempt to negotiate perspectives — all qualities emphasised about good teaching and learning — are also central to the kinds of processes we are engaged upon, and should be taken more seriously than they are. Conviction about process is necessary for meaningful consensus. Some years ago I was involved in research on the Standing Advisory Councils for Religious Education (probably some of you sit on such bodies). In pursuing their remit for Religious Education and Spiritual, Moral, Social and Cultural developments representatives of different faiths, with diverse and strongly held beliefs, need to find ways of agreeing how to apply their values and have them accommodated in educational endeavours. On the SACREs, however, especially in areas of high minority ethnic population, the minority faith representatives are marginalised, both in terms of the structure of the groups and often in the construction and conduct of the debates. Since the Education Reform Act of 1988 attention to cultural diversity and antiracism has declined in education: much remains to be done.

The SCAA Forum has given a positive national focus and high profile to values. Many people have said to me that they think this needs to be continued and sustained, not just given *ad hoc* attention. To an extent this is what VEC intends to do. But there is also a case for an ongoing Forum whose remit is to see how values issues can be considered in all subjects and across the curriculum. There is also a need to liaise with interest groups, as represented on Forum, who have close links with schools.

If we are serious about a quest for common values then it has to start with formal values education — Personal Social and Moral Education, Religious Education, citizenship — an underlying core of learning however labelled. In my personal opinion it is necessary for values education to have adequate and specific time in the timetabled curriculum and to be taught by teachers who are trained in the most appropriate strategies, such as discussion and small group work, and who are able to gain the confidence of students.

I believe there is a specific body of knowledge — philosophical, psychological and sociological — of which young people need to be aware, as well as developing the skills of moral reasoning, educating their emotions, building character and strengthening the moral will. We know from research and curriculum development over the last 25 years how some moral values education techniques work. But we still need much more specific research about the particular effects of certain strategies and contexts of teaching and learning in moral values education in order for schools and teachers to make informed decisions about what is appropriate for their schools. Complementary to this more focused work, are, of course, the learning climate as a whole and dealing with values issues in all areas of the curriculum. We need to aim for greater consistency and coherence in the implementation of values in schools and all our institutions.

Moving from the 'quest' to the 'common values' of the title of the seminar, this could at one level suggest the lowest common denominator. By contrast, I prefer the term and concept of 'shared' values, which implies working out, coming to an appreciation or even understanding, of other ways of thinking and feeling, of other world views — religious and non-religious. 'Shared' also indicates ownership, with some obligation to take responsibility to put the agreed values into practice and live by them. On the one hand, I see the quest as a journey, with the findings as provisional, open to criticism and review. On the other hand, the idea of common or even shared values appears either visionary, ideal, aspirational or stable, comfortingly reassuring — after all we all know about truth don't we?

Is it the values as such which are important or the attitudes held and the actions done in their name? And what about the reasons behind the actions or attitudes? Is it not just as important, possibly more so, to understand the reasons. When the same action is done for quite different reasons which are, in turn, related to values, to what extent does the value matter? For example, both sides in debate about capital punishment or abortion are likely to base their arguments on the value of human life.

The idea of common values also glosses over what is probably more common than generally acknowledged — the different priorities given to values in education and everyday life. By this I do not mean obvious conflicts of values, but variable weightings given to values according to different contexts or situations. For example, there can be justice or justice tempered by mercy or compassion. This is not the same as relativism, concern about which was the motivation for the SCAA initiative. (To my surprise Nick Tate also mentioned Marxism, a bogey which bedevilled Religious Education about 20 years ago; does it still exist?) Nor does the fact that we work with values priorities imply the need for absolute values — the desire of some politicians.

So what is common in terms of values? I prefer to start from everyday morality and particular cases in order to construct meaning making which is both personal and social. Moral panics raise the values profile. Certain events — the murder of James Bulger and of Philip Lawrence, Dunblane, machete attacks in the playground — become society's barometer. But it is not difficult to agree that such acts are wrong because they challenge our concept of what it is to be human. It is likely that there would also be common agreement about the immorality of recently reported cases such as: an 82 year-old woman peddling drugs to school children; a Scottish priest involved with pornography on the internet and alleged child abuse. These raise issues of trust and betrayal.

Moreover, there is usually common agreement that the quality of everyday life is impoverished by pervasive features such as dishonesty and vandalism, whether it be due to lack of care or intentional damage. The community forum of the parish council, on which I serve, frequently receives complaints of 'social disgrace' — children throwing stones, fireworks through letterboxes, tomato ketchup on cars, windows smashed. Why? In addition to the damage, which for the more vulnerable is psychological as well as material, victims have also to suffer the inadequacy and impotence of the police. Children and young people are much more aware of the limits of authority and of their 'rights'. Perhaps there has been too much emphasis on rights, not enough on corresponding responsibilities. How can the significance of community pressure be constructed and brought to bear? This has to come about by local will and a common willingness to discuss and take steps to improve the morality of the community. I am aware of projects in communities in the Netherlands where this has occurred.

Whilst it is fairly easy to describe the condition of society and even a measure of agreement about our common concerns, it is much more difficult to consider ways forward. This, I believe, is because there are several underlying insidious issues. One of these relates to coherence and integrity between public and private morality. Concerns are sometimes voiced about the example set by teachers. But what of the moral leadership of politicians and the captains of industry?

Also family values have been given much emphasis. It is widely assumed that all families are beneficent, and that all have families. Conflicts of values in the family are often ignored, whereas it is clear as a researcher, listening to young people, that much of the testing out of values occurs in the home and that here, too, values priorities occur. A friend, who takes a keen but critical interest in educational standards and the values debate, recently told me that it was easier to agree with her daughter and be supportive if the family wanted 'quality time together' rather than confrontation. I am not sure if she fully perceived the values choices she was making.

Family values and workplace values are mutually influential. We need to pay more attention to the interface of the personal and the professional and not treat them as separate realms. Values in each can be reinforcing or in tension.

There is also the issue of the relationship between majority and minority values. We are faced with a secular culture and the legacy of Christianity, together with religious diversity. Also aesthetic high and low cultures, about which we don't often speak these days. The dominant paradigm is always of a Christian society becoming multicultural. White British, for example, do not sufficiently reflect on what it is like to be, for example, a young Asian growing up in Britain, trying to make sense of at least two systems of cultural values , and probably to evolve a third by which to live. Humera Khan gave us some valuable insights in the discussion with earlier speakers.

These and other values issues — not least of economic values and their implications for the social framework — underly more overt attempts at seeking out common values.

In taking values considerations forward I would advocate that we pay more serious and genuine attention to the process — the quest for values: setting up — inclusion and exclusion; how the dialogue is conducted; the authenticity of the debate; checking perceptions and understandings; agreeing outcomes; allowing for ongoing revisions. School-based research shows that pupils value the process of valuing; listening, giving respect, demonstrating fairness.

The values of various groups, which vary according to their interests and purposes, is another issue needing more attention. We expect teachers to deal with complex values issues in the life of the school and in the curriculum. Yet they have virtually no training in this domain. Even when curriculum materials addressing the moral dimensions are available, the teacher is still the critical mediator, but may be required to adopt strategies differing from their usual subject teaching style. Indeed, we know very little about the values of teachers and their aims for values education in schools, or, indeed of whether these fit with the values of parents. Nick Tate seemed to be suggesting that in the SCAA consultation parents were questioning the fit. The police, media, music cultures are among other key influences on young people. More open debate about their guiding values is needed.

In conclusion, I should like to draw attention to the role of VEC as an ongoing network, forum for dialogue and source of support. As yet we are feeling our way. But during the next year we intend to compile a register of members and their interests and a speaker list; hold meetings and a conference; and work towards statements on certain values issues. To these ends we have currently set up sub-groups related to each of VEC's main aims. So, if you are interested to pursue today's questions further, especially in an educational context, join us! Those of us involved in VEC see the quest for values as lifelong, as an ongoing moral and spiritual journey. VEC's mission is both to give public recognition and significance to values issues and to attend to the moral development of adults as well as that of young people.

Presentation by

Professor Bhikhu Parekh
Department of Politics, University of Hull

My contribution will be more in the nature of reflections and notes on the current debate on common values. Basically, I intend to raise important questions rather than to attempt to answer them.

Firstly, when a topic becomes important and is placed on the public agenda there is always a political aspect to this development. So we need to ask ourselves why the issue of "common values" has suddenly become important as a public concern. The first question which arises is: why are we interested in common values? What do we want them for? In order to achieve what objectives? If we have managed to survive all these years without a debate on common values, what have we been missing and what is this gap that we are trying to fill?

Secondly, what do we mean by common values? What do we have in mind when we talk about "values"? For several centuries moral life was articulated in terms of ideals, principles, visions of the good, not in terms of values. If we look at the history of moral philosophy, we find that value has never been an important concept. The Greeks did not have a word for it. In Latin, value always meant value in an exchange. Value as a moral category is a peculiar product of modernity and brings all kinds of conceptual baggage with it. So why *do* we speak about common values and not in terms of a shared vision?

Thirdly, when we talk about *common* values, common in what sense? In the sense of a lowest common denominator, common in the sense of something which is shared? This implies that these values are grounded in specific traditions. These traditions are based on beliefs, but if you reflect upon them you might find that at a second order level they point to certain values and that these overlap between traditions. Is this what we have in mind when we talk about common values? Or are we thinking about some kind of moral universalism which is, as it were, reflected in different forms in different moral traditions? I wish to argue that this latter perspective is the wrong way of approaching the concept of common values, and that we have separate moral traditions which have grown up independently of each other. Our concern therefore is that, since different people draw their values from different moral traditions, we should explore if there are commonalities. What do exist are the Judaic tradition, the Hindu tradition, the Christian tradition, and so on. Each of these traditions has a specific set of values. Is it possible to find aspects, not so much common as *shared*, on which we can all agree?

Fourthly, if we can give some meaning to the concept of common values, at what level are we looking for common values? For example, you might look for common values at the personal level. How should I lead my own life as an individual? Is it possible to arrive at common values at this personal level? Or we might be looking for common values at the civil level: the way in which we interact with each other, for example the way that we conduct this meeting. After all, without *some* kind of shared values no dialogue is possible. Or are we thinking, not of values at the personal or social level, but at the collective and political level without which a common public life is impossible. Or, finally, are we talking about shared *spiritual* values, to which the SCAA report referred?

I am very sympathetic to the notion of spirituality although I have great difficulty in trying to make some sense of it! At one level we know that the spiritual goes beyond the moral and is not the same as the moral. But there is always a tendency for the spiritual to be appropriated by religious people, which is why the secularist and the atheist have seen this term as the thin end of the wedge! When we talk about the "spiritual", God is often brought into it with all the baggage of theology. Many of us, who may be uncomfortable with the concept of God, understood either in a personal way or in a theoretical sense, but who do have some feeling for this intermediate ground called spiritual, have often asked ourselves how we should define the "spiritual" in a manner that has no religious or theological overtones. What experience in my life is spiritual, but not religious or moral? To describe what experiences, what relationships, am I to use the word spiritual? I increasingly feel that there *are* experiences and relationships for which we need a set of values which are not moral and are not religious. But somehow we have lost that vocabulary of spirituality. Either we have lost it because the religious people and the theologians have put it to their own uses and have deprived the rest of us of it, or because we simply do not know what it means.

One of the concerns which I have is whether there is a vocabulary which is distinctively spiritual and which can unite people whether or not they are religiously inclined and, if so, how that vocabulary can be brought back into our life so that we can all say: Yes, we need that term because it plays an important role. For example, I can imagine a situation where I would use the term "sacred" for certain experiences or relationships. The Romans, for example, had the notion of piety, which did not involve a belief in God. One can have the notion of cosmic piety in the ecological debate without bringing in the notion of God. Or even, for example, the search for meaning in life. Or the idea of purity: the desire to be a pure, beautiful soul. Can I become a human being who is free from meanness, pettiness and jealousy? These notions go beyond morality, but they are not religious either.

Finally, are common values enough? Suppose we were all to agree on a body of common values. What would this settle? First of all, values do not bind a society together. Societies with shared common values can still fall apart. A classic example is Quebec in Canada. As long as Quebec was Catholic, it was one kind society. But in the '60s and '70s its values became profoundly different and increasingly like those of the rest of Canada. As Quebec became more like Canada, the secessionist movement there started because of the fear of becoming like "the Other". Why do secessions take place? Why do countries fall apart? Not because they fall out over values. You can share values and still profoundly disagree.

People can have shared values and still have disagreements. If you take the example of life as a value, immediately this raises half a dozen questions. What is life? When does it begin? And then you have the whole abortion debate. When does it end? And then you have the euthanasia debate. Or whose life? A person's life or an animal's life? There are Jains and others in India who would say that an animal's life is just as valuable as that of a human being. Again, people would say that although all human life is valuable, the more elevated life is of greater value because it can realise more human potential. Or, what does it mean to say that life is a value? What response is required from us? To cherish it, to see that it does not die? Or simply not to harm it? If I were to claim that life is a value, then it is not just a value here but everywhere else. Therefore I must commit myself to ensuring that life is preserved everywhere and in my own society as well. Again, we know that every year 40 old people die of hypothermia; we can predict this statistically. So are we holding life sacred if we do not prevent this? Are we holding life sacred when people commit suicide in prisons? So I am saying that if we agree on a common shared value of life, this is the *start* of the discussion and cannot be the end of it. It simply creates a shared moral universe in terms of which we are going to be mutually intelligible to one another. But the questions still arise. Is that life or not life? Whose life? And so forth.

Let me quickly try in the next few minutes to answer my own questions! First of all, why has the question of common values become important? The debate takes different forms in different countries. Everywhere it is concerned to deal with the challenge of plurality. Either it is an attempt to subvert plurality or it is an attempt to undergird it. In some cases there is a fear of plurality or diversity, whose existence is often attributed to immigrants. It is true that there is a plurality of values, but for the most part it has not been brought about by immigrants, who actually share most of the values of the society to which they have come. Plurality has come about because of the internal disintegration of our society. But one sees cultural plurality and one begins to panic, and look for common values.

The notion of common values can also become a subversive way of undermining cultural plurality. When Mrs Thatcher was concerned with the Victorian values of making Britain great, this was a way of saying that only those cultural differences would be tolerated which were in harmony with a specific set of shared common values. There is therefore a ground for the suspicion that the concern with common values is designed to undermine plurality. But there is also another side to the common values debate. We may start by *accepting* plurality, but ask how much plurality should be tolerated. At what point should we be able to say that certain practices are not acceptable? And, equally importantly, how can we create bridges to cope with plurality, such that people can talk to each other, trust each other and count on each other through their common bond of shared values?

So common values can come in either as a stealthy and subtle way of undermining cultural plurality or as a way of undergirding it. The first is a non-starter and I do not believe it will work. I propose that when we think of common values we think of them as providing a framework within which cultural plurality can flourish.

Let us now turn to the second question. What do we mean by values and by common values? The answer to this difficult question could take an hour, but I shall try to deal with it very briefly. As an example, is monogamy a value or a practice? Lots of Muslims and other people would say that monogamy is a practice which is common in this society and if you want to live here you follow it, but that it is not a value. Many young people today would also describe monogamy as a practice rather than a value. In other words, what can be a value for one person may be a practice for another. A value is a way of internally appropriating, of internally relating to a practice. I might follow monogamy as a practice but I might not throw myself into that practice in a wholehearted way and cherish it as a value. So when we talk about values, we are not just talking about practices, but about appropriating those practices in a certain manner.

So, crudely, let me say that by values I mean those things which are for us worth cherishing and worth living up to. Talk about values is ultimately talk about what kind of life is worth living. Values are neither given, in the sense of being objective, nor in the sense of being merely preferences. They are values *for us*; nothing can be a value for you unless you can see the point of it. Monogamy would be just a practice and would not be a value unless you began to internalise it. Values, by their very nature, are not "out there". They are the fruits of intersubjective deliberation arrived at by a specific community. Some values might be common to a particular group or a society; some might be common to humanity as a whole. In our talk of common values, the higher we go in the level of generality, the thinner these values become.

At what level are we seeking common values? Common values are absolutely crucial at the political level because it relates to our shared life. A society's values are embodied in a framework of law that is binding on us all. When a law is made we cannot evade it and the values behind it are enforced on us. When law is involved we have to share a common value. Once we move beyond that civil level to a personal level, values have to allow for a greater deal of freedom of interpretation and a great deal of diversity. The Australian Commission on Multi-Cultural Society said that the rule of law, equality of the sexes, freedom of speech, freedom of religion and the obligation to obey the law are the common public values of Australian society and Australians are required to cherish them. The task of a public institution is to make sure that those values which are central to the public life of a community are sustained. Beyond that values should not be the concern of the government.

Are values enough? There are two things to bear in mind here. When we talk about values this is never enough. Values are like pawns on a chess board. I may believe in liberty, equality and justice but just to do so of itself takes me nowhere. Values have to be *applied* and then they conflict. I cannot think of any two values that do not conflict and since they conflict, their application necessarily requires a certain moral skill: skill, as in a game of chess, in how to define

44

values and how to relate them. So when we talk about values we must also talk about cultivating appropriate moral skills. At a deeper level the spiritual dimension is relevant. Why should we follow these values? How can I persuade someone that they should be living by these values: values which require the sacrifice of self-interest, which we are not inclined to do? What drives me to follow them? For a religious person the answer is easy: God sees everything and I cannot hide from Him. The non-religious person should look at the classic writers such as Plato, Aristotle and Cicero who invoke "love of the good". Why should I follow these values? Because I want to be a good human being. Unless these values are grounded in "love of the good", they have no energy or strength and are easily set aside. The question for us in educating children, at home or in school, is how to endow them with moral skills, which will enable them to use values as a moral compass with which to navigate their way through life and how to cultivate in them "love of the good". Values give us the criteria for moral judgements; they give us spectacles through which to analyse situations and then to apply our moral skills to them.

Lastly, I feel even more strongly about the content of values. If we look at the debate on values we see that there are two dominant tendencies in the history of the Western world. One is what I call "moral monism", that is, the assumption that only one way of life is the best, whether Greek, Christian or whatever. You are not leading a good life if you do not follow it and all other ways of life are rejected. The other difficulty has been the persistent strand of rationalism, with reason seen as the highest faculty against which other things do not count. Therefore, if you look at the whole list of values on which we have concentrated they are trapped within these two traditions. So we talk about self-criticism, impartiality, truth, respect for differences. All of them are values at a distance.

Our list of values has to be relevant to our times; values cannot be stationary. Looking at our times, what are the values that need to be emphasised? To me the experience of the Holocaust, of Bosnia and of all the painful tragedies of our time is the context for determining the content of our values. Given that this is the context, what are the values that we ought to be fostering and are the values which are traditionally stressed enough? Although they are useful in some respects, they are ultimately inadequate. If we recognise that we live in a culturally plural world, what are the values that are central to that world? Not just *respect* for differences. We need to go beyond that. We need *love* of diversity. Not just the fact that I acknowledge that you are a Jew and that you go to a synagogue, but that I delight in the fact that you are different from me and that you have something to contribute to the moral conversation which goes on in our shared life. Therefore I want you to be what you are. I do not want to assimilate you, because I would then lose you and your distinctive voice. Therefore *respect* for diversity is not enough: what we need is *love* of diversity.

There is no reference to this in much of the literature. Western civilisation has cultivated different virtues from those stressed by the Indian or the Chinese. Hindus, for example, would talk about non-violence, but the Jewish tradition has a different set of virtues. This is what is wonderful about diversity: that because human values conflict and human capacities differ, different civilisations have cultivated different virtues. Can we bring these values together and learn from each other, swapping virtues and learning from each others' traditions? One of the greatest virtues is humility, which requires me to concede that my values are not the final word. That is why one of the greatest vices of modernity is self-righteousness: the conviction that only the modern way of doing things is the best. But, if modern liberal civilisation is the best, how could the Holocaust happen, and not just happen as a result of the actions of a madman, but with the rest of the Western world quietly watching? So in a sense it indicts not just Germany, but European civilisation; it happened in the centre of Europe, while Europe was watching. How could this happen? What made it possible? Why do we not recognise that these events require us to take a deeper and more critical look at European civilisation? I would suggest that in order to arrive at common values, at shared values, we need to take a radical, critical look at the fundamental assumptions of our civilisations and try to foster the virtues of tenderness, gentility and humility.

All our values tend to be centred around the operation and cultivation of reason. But what about virtues relating to our emotions, such as compassion, which is a key strand in Buddhism. Compassion also plays an enormously important role in Judaism and in Christianity, in terms of love of one's fellow human beings and love of the world, what in Latin is called the "amor mundi": that is, I love this world and I want it to flourish. When we talk about values we should think about values of the emotions as well and conduct our debate from within the context of the tragedies of our time and the light these throw on the limits of our civilisation and on where we need to go from here. Values are not given. They have to be created; and created in the light of what we believe to be the historical experience of mankind and the needs of our age.

*   *   *

Questions and discussion following Professor Bhikhu Parekh's Presentation

Ms Humera Khan: I am concerned that at inter faith meetings we often spend too much time in secular deliberations. Too often people from faith communities experience situations in which they are not able to express themselves as they would wish. Perhaps in the discussion so far there has been a tendency to go along too much with what is "politically correct". We find ourselves in a unique time in our history when people can travel from one end of the earth to the other within a day. This is a new situation and we have to accept responsibility for the way in which we respond to it. The real crisis in many ways is one of identity. We need to be able to affirm our identities and not be frightened of doing so. In particular we need to own our particular religious perspectives even though it may be out of fashion to do so.

Ms Zerbanoo Gifford: I agree strongly that it is important to recognise the significance of our emotional as distinct from rational qualities. There is a risk that we go on just talking about values; in my work with young people I find that they are interested in *action* rather than talk. Schools need to address such issues as the exploitation of child labour around the world. There are issues of this kind which concern children on which we need to take a stand.

Professor Bhikhu Parekh: As a result of the way our vocabulary has evolved we talk a lot about "truth". But truth can be seen in fifty different ways. Earlier writers did not talk about propositional "truth". They saw truth as *veritas,* as a virtue. The Greeks thought in terms of discovering the characteristics of the world around them. Truth in our day has acquired a scientific ring and it is seen as being objective. But this is an incomplete understanding of it. We need to make sure that our vocabulary resonates with our experience.

Dr Manazir Ahsan: In your presentation you have almost demolished the concept of "values"! You have talked about "the truth" But who is going to tell us what is truth and what is not truth? Where on the basis of the position you have described are we to find any arbiter? From your perspective, how are we to define the "good" and how do we get to that "truth"?

Professor Bhikhu Parekh: There are many fundamental questions here! When I introduced the notion of "love of the good" it was for a specific purpose. In most debates on values there is a tendency simply to reinforce the positivism of our age. These things, we say, are good; and other things are bad. But then we find we no longer agree on these. This is precisely what is wrong with the debate. I can draw up a list of virtues such as compassion and humanity. But I do not know what the "truth" would mean. Morality is not a matter of "truth". I can argue that my values are more rational and more defensible than yours and I can try to show you that your values are untenable. But even if I were to convince you that this is the case, what would give you the motive and energy to live out your life in terms of those values? People are tempted to cheat. Why should I not do so? What stops me? Morality always makes demands on us. Where do we get the strength to respond to these demands? When I am tempted to cut corners, why should I not do so? What drives me? From where does my moral life get its energy and tenacity? Religious people get it from God because they live out their morality out of a love of God. Gandhi said that the difference between a moral man and a spiritual man is the difference between an honest mercenary and an ardent patriot. They may behave exactly the same, but one is more reliable and is more energised.

As I am not a religious person in the traditional sense of the term, but in the Roman sense in which religion connects you to others and to the universe, or in the Buddhist sense, the question for me is what gives my moral life its energy and force? I would say "love of the good". I would not dream of doing certain things because I am not that kind of person. I would not cheat because I know that it would diminish me. We need that kind of nourishing soil which I would call the spiritual if we are to live a moral life. This is not a moral issue, for it goes beyond ideas of right and wrong.

When you ask how I know that my values are better than yours, there is obviously a big debate. But we do not begin history from scratch. People have thought about these matters, and have come to the conclusion that the good life needs to be lived out in a certain way. For there is in practice a consensus on this. Consensus is a filtering process through the collective trial and error of humanity, through experimentation and reflection on historical experience, as a result of which certain moral conclusions are reached. I would therefore start from a consensually grounded group of values and not by asking *de novo* what is good. From within that corpus of values, with what do I feel sympathy? Values conflict and then what do I do? How do I live out my values in my life? I need to relate them to my history and to my circumstances. That is our problem and task, rather than simply to define what is good.

Rt Revd Gavin Reid

**Anglican Bishop of Maidstone, Chair of the Archbishops'
Millennium Advisory Group and Deputy Moderator of the
Churches Together in England Working Party on the Millennium**

In the light of the Chief Rabbi's comments this morning, I would like to emphasise that the Church of England is not a "state church". It may be a *national* Church, but it is not a "state church". Indeed, some of the problems and tensions during the last 20 years have arisen just because the State is beginning to realise that the Church of England does not intend to be a "state church". A national Church has a different role and, of course, a national Church can lose its franchise! That may be an interesting possibility to contemplate. I do not myself think the Church should give up this role but it certainly could lose it.

First, a story that will give you an idea of where where I am coming from. Some years ago the Archbishop of Canterbury made a speech which dealt with relationships between Christians and Muslims. The BBC in its wisdom (or lack of it) invited myself and a spokesman for the Muslim faith to take part in a morning programme. When we arrived in the coffee lounge beforehand, both of us knew the game that was going to be played. We both knew that what was likely to happen was that they would try to set us at loggerheads with each other, so we decided to get our act together in the coffee room before we went in. We identified the areas of common ground between us. One thing we agreed that was common between the two of us was that we both wanted to share and commend our faith to the other. When we do that, we create an open situation in which anything might happen. I do not want to be part of the kind of society that has a "politically correct" multi-faith philosophy that says you cannot share your faith with others. I do not want to go along with the notion that because the other person may be impressionable you avoid talking to them about what is precious to you. That is an area of tension that I think I have to be honest about and share with you before I go any further.

When I was invited to come to this seminar I was just beginning to talk with people in the Inter Faith Network about the Churches' plans for the Millennium because it is extremely important to us to be doing so, and that is why I am here today. Throughout this morning I have been wanting to revise and change and throw out everything I have brought along to say but I am not going to do so.

I am going to focus on the "mechanics" of promoting "mega debates".

As you know, the Churches have suggested that a major national debate on values should be promoted, linked to the Millennium. I would like to offer some reflections on whether, if you want to do so, you can actually say something of significance in our kind of society so that everybody hears it. How do you conduct a great debate in a society, in a nation? Is it even possible to do so? The Millennium Churches' Group which I serve is going about the Millennium, for shorthand purposes, in two ways. We see the Millennium as both a kind of "mega Christmas" and a kind of "mega New Year's Eve".

I have little doubt that the year or so before the magic 2000 comes into the diary will be a prolonged psychological New Year's Eve. The media will almost certainly help this along with various reflective articles about the past and about the future. We may have a more reflective society on our hands than we have known for generations and it is an appropriate time to be asking "What are the new century resolutions?".

I think it would be foolish not to seize on a national mood of reflection. We do not live in a very reflective society. It is over pragmatic and overdosed with the present. To actually take stock about the past and look for visions for the future is a tremendous opportunity and, in this, Christians will find that they are not the only people with hopes and dreams for the future and thoughts about the past. If a "mega debate" is to be effectively launched in our country, I am sure it would be right for it to come from a broad-based platform, including those of Christian faith, those of other faiths and those who may profess to have no faith whatsoever.

In terms of the "mega Christmas", obviously the particular calendar which we use in this country and which happens to say that we are near to the year 2000, is a Christian calendar. It was created by Christians based on calculations (that we now know are probably at least four years out!) about the birth of Christ and was imposed on this country by the Synod of Whitby, a national Church occasion which predated any national civil parliament.

It is understandable in a country where, in a recent Gallup poll, (and you might be surprised to learn this), 77% of those interviewed could name a Christian denomination with which they recognised some sort of personal or at least family link, and in a country where the head of state is also the symbolic Supreme Governor of the Church of England that the Churches should want to do all they can to make the connnection in the public mind between the year 2000 and the fact and significance of Jesus Christ.

My first encounter with representatives of the Government and of the Millennium Commission to talk about the Millennium was over a year ago. My opening question was: "How much are you taking on board in your plans that the Millennium is a Christian festival?" To this the answer was:"That's an interesting thought". The second response was that to do so would marginalise other faiths and that could be problematic. That was why I had to make contact with people from other faith communities, whom I now deeply respect, who have met with us a couple of times, and I hope will meet with us more times, in order to maintain a process of ensuring we do *not* marginalise people of other faiths.

Whether we like it or not there is a link between religion and values, and the remarkably large proportion of the population that holds a nominal religious position are linked predominantly to the Christian religious tradition. So we shall need to be quite up front about the story that lies at the heart of that tradition and to which the Millennium is linked.

Here you might be surprised to learn that the Churches are in great need of help from our friends in other faith communities. If I may say so, the Chief Rabbi's talk this morning was extremely helpful to me in its methodology. There is a real danger of triumphalism and religious insensitivity on the part of Christians, the majority religious strand in this country, who are often totally blind to the effects they can have in this respect. The Churches do not want to mark the Millennium in ways that cause distress to other faith groups.

But there is another way in which we need the help of other faiths. There is a growing "politically correct" philosophy about a multi-faith society, with which I have yet to find a serious adherent of another faith agree. It is an approach which says that everybody must play down their religious distinctions and convictions. "Isn't that what was wrong in Bosnia, Northern Ireland and so on?", it is said. Because of this view, which has permeated Government thinking, we need the goodwill and the understanding (and almost the permission) of our friends in the other faiths to tell our Christian story in a major way and to make our point strongly to Government at both local and national levels. I cannot say how helpful we found the recent "Thought for the Day" by Indarjit Singh. He had the freedom, through being a Sikh, to remind this country that the Millennium has a Christian point to it. He could say that far more powerfully than we Christians could,and he did so.

I would now like to look at some of the factors which we have to bear in mind when we think about the techniques of promoting public debates. You may actually think that we do not *want* to engage in a "mega-debate" about values linked to the Millennium. That is an open question. I am not totally convinced about it at this stage, although I am still commited to it as a proposal that the Churches want to explore.

It is an astonishing irony that we live in an age of rapid advance in terms of the means of communication and yet at the same time we live in an age where very few people feel that their voices are heard. We no longer live in communicative societies. The well and the market place have been replaced by the impersonal tap which de-socialises the fetching of water and the supermarket that de-socialises the fetching of food. Rumours are not spreading from mouth to mouth but from hoarding to hoarding. This means that he who can hire the hoarding controls the conversation. I have a daughter and son-in-law in the advertising business so I am well briefed about it!

As someone who has watched the powerful flow of false perceptions about the Church of England coming from the popular press in recent years, I find the whole thing really quite frightening. There is no structured right of reply. Whenever I have been able to exercise a right of reply it is in a tiny letter in the letter columns, at which the reader does not look anyway.

We all know that in spite of the well meaning sounds that come from Government, the press and television tend to fall into relatively few controlling hands. Television is particularly disturbing because it purports to present the viewer with visual reality. You believe what you see, but no one sees the editor who decides which way the camera points, what footage is used and what footage is discarded. To echo a greater person's words: "Never in the field of human discourse has so much been said to so many by so few."

Faced with this communicational disenfranchising of the many, there are two disturbing responses which suggest themselves to those considering engagement in a national debate. The first is that you accept that there is nothing that the individual can do. You give up and you settle for the role of consumer and spectator. The second is to organise events and happenings that are so momentous that they cannot fail to attract media attention. The latter strategy can appear to be a way of "making free speech happen", but it can also lead to the brutal tactics of an IRA "seeking the oxygen of publicity."

If we are to stimulate a national debate in a modern society, we have to remember that the biggest fact of life is that the media is owned by a minority. So either we get the press barons to agree that our agenda for the debate is important; and even better, has sales value for them or we organise the debate on such a scale that they cannot risk missing the stories about it we create. These are the choices before us if we want to try to stimulate a big debate on values in our society.

I would like, now, to draw some lessons from the past. I am not going to talk about the way in which debates spring up off the back of a Dunblane or following Mrs Lawrence's recent initiative in speaking out about moral values. (To be frank it is early days yet, but the Scots cynicism in me says that at the moment all this is a news item and not a debate. When another more interesting news item comes along that will be the end of it).

So what are the lessons to be learned from the past? I can think of two attempts in the 1970's of the Churches to mount a national debate relating to morals and values. There are lessons to be learnt from both of them, mainly negative ones.

The first initiative was in 1971, the *"Festival of Light"*, which some of you may just remember. This stemmed from the vision which a young Christian worker returning from overseas work had when he saw the values of his own country with a fresh eye. He was particularly shocked by what he called "moral pollution" which related especially to pornography and the portrayal of sexual mores on television and in the cinema.

In the space of a relatively few months, an astonishingly strange combination of forces came together: first of all, the charismatic Evangelical Christian community, (very much dragging the rest of the Church by the nose, and convinced that God was calling them to act prophetically); second, Mary Whitehouse and the "Moral Rearmament" lobby, which had for some time engaged with an agenda, of "cleaning up television"; third, Malcolm Muggeridge, who was a constituency of his own, driven by a kind of world-weary feeling, and perhaps even guilt driven, in reaction against what he felt was the pollution of our culture; and fourth, (and how they got into this still amazes me), the American "Jesus Movement", especially represented by a particular individual called Arthur Blessit, who somehow saw this as a stepping stone to getting into Britain as a mission field.

All these different ingredients came together and it was in consequence an astonishing event. Within months, rallies had taken place, and beacons were being lit all over the country. Thousands of teenagers were seen all over the place with slogans in support of the cause written on their T-shirts. There were meetings in Westminster Central Hall, Trafalagar Square and Hyde Park, pulling in huge crowds and the media reported it all at some length. There was a tremendous feeling that at last the people had spoken, the silent majority had reared up, was saying what it had long wanted to say and was being given the opportunity to do so.

But 25 years later the Festival of Light can be seen to have achieved very little in regard to the moral values of the nation, if measured against its own goals. It certainly provided a fillip for charismatic Christianity and stimulated a British replica of the Jesus Movement. It left behind a lobbying organisation called CARE which in my judgement still does a number of good things. But I do not think that the movement as a whole really made much impact on the nation or reduced the level of "moral pollution" as they had identified it.

The fact of the matter was that there were two if not three different agendas being pursued by people who had very little in common. The dynamism came from the Churches but they were represented mainly from the Evangelical wing. They were torn between promoting a moral debate and calling people to repentance and faith in Christ. If you are Evangelical, and I am, you will always find it almost irresistible to pursue the second in preference to the first. There was little attempt to make common cause with those of other faiths or those who had similar concerns in the area of sexual morality, and morality itself was narrowed down to an area of personal sexual behaviour, which I do not want left out for one moment but which is not the whole of the moral agenda.

Secondly, I want to consider the Archbishop's *"Call to the Nation"*. On October 15 1975 the then Archbishop of Canterbury, Dr Coggan, took to the airwaves to launch this. When he had come to office some months earlier many had written to him urging him to call the nation to prayer, to give a lead to the nation that was seen to be falling apart morally and many were saying that time was short and that something needed to be done. He wondered whether the way to launch the cause was through great statements on great occasions in cathedrals up and down the country. But in the end he planned a campaign based on a direct personal appeal through the media. So the television cameras, the radio reporters and the press were there in strength at Lambeth Palace on 15 October 1975. Such was the level of professionalism of Lambeth Palace at the time (not at all like it is today!) that nobody had checked whether the fuses would cope with the surge when the TV lights went on. I have been told that they could not and that they blew! Much of the TV coverage of the key launching moment was lost! In a sense, this blew the whole initiative.

Dr Coggan's Call was based on five phrases which are worth comparing with the values in the SCAA document we have been examining. The five phrases were: *Each man and woman matters; the family matters; good work matters; the other fellow matters;* and *attitudes matter.* Two questions were posed. *What sort of society do we want* and *what sort of people do we need in order to achieve it?* The high profile national call was well reported and the leaders in the press and much of the public comment was friendly and positive. There was a lot of initial support for the Call and the politicians were no doubt jumping on the band wagon.

It was followed by a pastoral letter to be read in all the churches. That letter attempted to mobilise the churches to support what had actually already been started but about which they had not been told in advance. It suggested putting together structures to respond to people's reactions to the Call and in a way it revealed just how top down the whole initiative had been in its conception. The immediate measure of the Call's effectiveness was some 27,000 letters: there is not a great deal of evidence that anything else was achieved as a result of it.

If in 1999 we are to mount a national debate on moral values as the Churches have suggested then the experience of past attempts to do so perhaps bring us little encouragement. The Churches have not yet begun their detailed thinking about 1999 and 2000. There are, however, a few thoughts in my mind which I should like to share with you as I close.

The first point is that the time is more propitious in 1999 than it was in 1971 or 1975. I believe that there is every possibility that the sense of an era coming to an end, and an awareness of a unknown future ahead will create a more thoughtful mood in the public at large. New Year's Eve is often a sobering time, at least before the corks are popped! I think it will be important to work with the dynamics of a "mega New Year's Eve", the natural dynamics of which will encourage stocktaking and the identification of hopes and aspirations.

Secondly, I think we need to identify what we want to say and to debate in terms of specifics rather than generalities. Dr Coggan's Call was about generalities. I admit that the *Festival of Light* was much more about specifics but it was in fact cast in very broad terms.

Thirdly, we need to work from a broad based platform rather

than keeping the debate as the preserve of the Churches. That is why, I suppose, that I accepted the invitation to be here today.

Fourthly, we need to talk with the media moguls and seek their help and not just assume that they are not interested. Let me tell you a hitherto unknown story. Some of you may know that I worked in the 1980's with Dr Billy Graham. I directed his two great missions of 1984/85 and 1989 and I found it a very interesting time. One of the reasons why I believe in the value of what we did was that he created a sufficient splash to make people take notice of his agenda and this was important. The by-product was almost more important than the product. I believed in the product but I believed even more in the by-product, because in an unreflective society there is a need to crash through into the awareness of people to make them reflect on important areas of life.

In the middle of the 1989 mission I was informed that Dr Graham wanted me to accompany him to a lunchtime engagement. This had been arranged by Rupert Murdoch, who had flown in at high speed, had called together all his editors and had got in touch with Conrad Black and made sure that all the Telegraph editors and also the big Chief of the Daily Mail would be there too, and also David Dimbley. The lunch had been arranged to hear Dr Graham talking about what mattered to him and what lay behind the lunch was a sense of "We ought to get behind this". I fight hard against a natural cynicism, but nevertheless I believe that it is worthwhile to make the effort to reach the leaders of the media. You should assume that such people are not disinterested before you discover they are. They may not have different agendas but if the end product is exposure for, and facilitating of, the debate which you think is important, then that is good enough for me.

Fifthly, we need to have our constituencies alerted beforehand so that they are ready to take part and that a call to a national debate is backed by local structures and activities already in a position for people to talk with each other, to share and to listen.

Sixthly, I believe we need to construct the debate in concrete rather than in abstract terms. The danger of all moral debates is that they are no more than word games. Perhaps it might be better if we focused on a number of specific projects which embody the values that we want to commend. These could be projects already taking place, or projects specifically set up to make the point. Such projects might include, for example, taking on board the Old Testament principle of Jubilee, joining with those of other faiths and of none in calling for the remission of international debts where they are clearly crippling small nations in other parts of the world.

Also, in supporting Jubilee projects in our own country, such as seeking to end homelessness, especially among the young. We could highlight people in groups who are proving on the ground that they can create community or bring ethnic groups together or improve the environment.

Seventhly, we need to learn from the advertising industry how to "spread rumours" in today's world and how to create an awareness that something is happening. I do not believe that you can use the techniques of advertising to convert anybody to anything. That is why I am interested in advertising, because you can actually use it to raise questions and to facilitate a discussion.

So at the end of the debate about the debate, I fully expect that most if not all of my ideas will get blown away. But I do hope that we are left with something other than the defeatist proposition that there is, after all, nothing that we can do!

*　　*　　*

Questions and discussion following Presentation by Bishop Gavin Reid

Dr Helen Haste: You have been reflecting on an approach which might be taken as encouraging a Christian moral revivalism. You have referred to your concern to involve other faith communities in the proposed debate. To what extent are you ready to include in your project those who hold a secular position?

Rt Revd Gavin Reid: First of all, the term Christian revivalism is not one which I used. But, secondly, I referred to the danger of Christian triumphalism and the need to avoid this. Thirdly, I think that "secular" does not necessarily have to mean the opposite of "religious". It is possible to use the word secular in the sense of a faith position and indeed there can be certain liberating aspects found in secular philisophy. Everyone needs something in which they can place their faith (whether this is a religious tradition or a philosophical position). Otherwise we would not get out of bed in the morning!

Revd. I O Smith: I live and work in east London as a Christian and community leader.

We need to think of ways in which we can help to sustain our communities at grass-root level, both the young and the old, and to educate people to understand and appreciate each other's values. Too often our faith traditions have become buried in our society.

Making my way in Britain I would have been lost in the crowd if I had not had the values derived from my faith, which are my strength. We need to be ready to face change but we also need to value the resources on which we have been able to depend. For example, I have had a settee for 15 years. I do not want to change it because it is strong and beautifully made. I prefer to keep what I have been able to enjoy and trust. It is important that people should hold fast to what is good.

Children in school are constantly faced with conflicting messages on what they should believe. They are faced with the rapid increase of crime in our society and the emphasis placed on sex, drugs, sport and entertainment. We need to develop the moral strength of children and young people to help them to swim against this tide. We also need to help people understand different faiths and the values which they uphold. There are those within my community who are reluctant to enter into dialogue with people of other faiths because they do not understand and appreciate them and we need to consider how to address their concern.

General Discussion in Closing Session

Mr Brian Pearce: Perhaps at this stage we should broaden out our discussion. We included some questions on today's agenda for us to address in this session without wanting to narrow the focus of the discussion to these. There are two areas on which it would be helpful for us to focus and they overlap. First, is it realistic to suppose that within a plural society there can be a shared understanding of the nature of values and morality? Is the quest for common values a necessary and valid one? Then we should perhaps move on to deal with some of the issues raised by the presentations from Dr Tate and Bishop Gavin Reid about the processes involved in taking these kind of issues forward within our present day society.

Dr N.K. Prinja: Throughout the day we have heard speakers using a variety of terms: common values, shared values, morals, codes of conduct, duties and rights. Within the Hindu tradition we have a single term which embraces all of these concepts: Dharma. For us the present debate about values is not new; it has been going on for many centuries. The Hindu tradition is perhaps the oldest living faith and there are as many different religious perspectives contained within it as there are outside it. It is the overarching concept of Dharma which has kept these different strands within the unity of a single framework.

Dharma means the natural eternal laws which are applicable to everyone and to the whole universe. However, there is a recognition that the implication and the application of these laws will change from time to time and from place to place. That is one reason why the Hindu tradition has survived: it has allowed freedom of expression and thought in interpreting these universal laws and accommodating, for example, the discoveries of science and technology so that from the Hindu viewpoint there is no need for conflict between science and religion.

As civilisations develop and our understanding of the world in which we live improves, we find that we deepen our knowledge of Dharma and its eternal and universal laws. Whether these are called moral values, shared values, righteousness or a code of conduct, it is important for people to have the freedom to interpret them and to apply them in the way which suits their circumstances. This enables people to maintain their own identities. At the same time, they have to recognise in turn the right of others to maintain *their* identities. It is difficult for an approach of this kind to be successful if it based on a single book, a single set of rules, a single prophet or a single messenger. There is a need for a framework of values which is universal but one which is not applied rigidly.

Rabbi Jacqueline Tabick: In Judaism we have a Festival of Passover. There are four questions which Jewish children learn and ask as part of the Passover ritual. One bright child asked me once: "Why is it important to learn these questions? Surely, it is the answers that we need to know!". Perhaps a way forward is to acknowledge the importance of our having common questions. In her talk, Monica Taylor talked about the importance of process. As I see it, asking questions and having the humility to listen to the answers and being able to realise that the answer we hear is only the starting point for fresh questions lies at the heart of the process. The debate on common values is in itself of great importance. I would be anxious if we tried to draw up a fixed list of values. What we need is a process of continuing refinement of our values as a result of shared debate and dialogue and at each stage we should see the possibility of another level of understanding emerging.

Rabbi Dr Julian Jacobs: Discussions of the kind we are having today can be of limited value in their impact on society. After we leave, what will we have achieved in making our society better? I would perhaps question whether there *can* be "common values". Even if everyone in this room agrees on a particular value that does not mean that others outside it are going to agree . Throughout the world we are all influenced by the different cultures from which we come and people have different values. Even if you take the sanctity of human life which may seem a common denominator you find that this has different gradations in society. On the whole, the Jewish and Christian traditions which have greatly influenced the Western world hold human life to be of greater value than perhaps do some other societies. And again, some people may be blessed with a very high moral standard, but others may not be.

Therefore the search for common standards and values seems to be a problematic goal. What we regard as common values others might think to be of no importance. So we must focus on more practical questions: our society is in such a state that we need to do this. The Jewish faith has a simple rule of thumb, which others have as well, "What is hateful to you, do not do to others". Everyone understands this principle and we need to concentrate on commending it within our own communities and within society as a whole.

Mrs Ivy Gutridge: Wolverhampton Inter Faith Group started 22 years ago and the position has changed a good deal since then. At that time there were many Christians who thought that it was inconsistent with the Christian faith to be involved in inter faith dialogue. We have made good progress towards understanding one another better. 22 years ago the situation in Wolverhampton was a bad one, with racial disturbances and a prejudiced press. The local churches came together to explore what it meant in practical terms to love your neighbour if they are of another faith and concluded that they must support their neighbour on their own faith journey. We all have misconceptions about each other, even after we have been involved in inter faith dialogue for a number of years. We must take every possible opportunity to dispel these misconceptions and to remain in dialogue with one another. The Millennium provides us with a good opportunity to focus on the need to understand one another better.

Most Ven. Dr M Vajiragnana: In Buddhism, our values are based on our physical life, our mental life and our working life. If any of our actions bring harm to ourselves or to others then these are considered to be bad. If any actions bring peace and happiness they are considered good. In the current debate we are trying to understand what may be our common values and to decide what is right and what is wrong. According to the Buddhist tradition good and evil arise according to our intentions and the consequences of our thoughts and actions. We are taught that in our actions we should to seek to help everyone and to practice kindness in action and in words. We can talk theoretically about common values for many hours but what are their practical implications? In Buddhism we believe that our own home is the place in which to start practising these values and then in the wider society. As the Chief Rabbi said in his presentation, we can use schools and our temples, synagogues, churches and mosques as places in which children are taught to imbibe their respective values and to be helpful and kind to others.

It is even more important today to inculcate these attitudes from early childhood. Sadly, many criminals are of a young age and this is because they are not taught or shown by example either at home or in school to be kind and to practise love. They think that they can do what they want, so they hurt others, doing cruel things and sometimes even killing. Kindness needs to be taught to children in the home and in the school. It is important to use gentle and not harsh words. Children can be coarsened through the use of harsh language. I remember when someone asked a small girl in my presence what was her name. "Shut up, Helen" she said. She was asked again and she said "Shut up Helen" again. She thought that was her name because of the way in which she was used to being addressed in her home. Children need to be taught by example, by their families and by their teachers.

In the Buddhist tradition we are taught to respect our parents and our teachers. In thinking about how we teach these values we need to bear in mind that in schools children are taught these days about many different religions. In doing this, it is important not to emphasise one particular religion more than another or to tell children that one is better than the others. Rather it is better to emphasise that all religions believe that kindness and tolerance are important and these can be seen as an common values for us all.

Revd Marcus Braybrooke: The question has been raised as to why we need to discuss the question of common values and about the practical value of doing so. At the 1993 World Parliament of Religions in Chicago many leading members of the different world faiths added their names to the Declaration on a Global Ethic. This document attempted to respond to the critical issues facing our world and the opening session of the Parliament began with a review of them. The Declaration itself says "The world is in agony, peace eludes us, the planet is being destroyed, neighbours live in fear, women and men are estranged from each other . . . children die" It was hoped at Chicago that the attempt to enunciate shared values would lead into common action and those at the Parliament were appealing for common action by those of different faiths to redress what is wrong with our world. The need to establish a link between values and practice is obviously important.

I hope also that in our discussions together we will be self critical. Some of those values which I would like to see implemented have not always been upheld by the religions, for example, in their record on ecology, on human rights, and on relations between men and women. There is a need in the debate for a note of penitence and self-criticism on the part of our religious communities.

Mr Indarjit Singh: I see the Millennium as an excellent opportunity for stocktaking. It happens to be a special anniversary in the Christian calendar, but it also provides an opportunity for all of us to reflect on what has gone wrong in our society. I hope that the opportunity to do this will be grasped.

I feel our society has taken a wrong direction and is over obsessed with self; it has put too much emphasis on the autonomy of individuals and shows a lack of concern for the effect that this can have on others. Every night television advertisements appeal to the viewers' greed and their desire for instant gratification and "quick fixes" and the encouragement of these attitudes is causing great problems in our society. We see their impact at its most extreme in cases of children murdering children. We are alerted to our society's problems by such major tragedies as the shooting in Dunblane, but then we too easily forget about them again as the next news story takes over. We need to look very hard at where we are going as a society and the impact of excessive individualism on it. Today, in place of the traditional marriage contract, with the acceptance of its obligations "for richer, for poorer, in sickness or in health", society thinks that as long as two people show superficial love, that is enough. But then they split up and their children suffer. I see this increasingly in the youth court on which I serve. Well over 90% of the children appearing there come from broken homes. Only yesterday we had before us in court a child who had been causing criminal damage. What was his background? His parents had separated and his stepfather had sexually abused him. What hope does that child have?

There is a good deal for us to be ashamed about in our society. If we want to change the direction in which society is heading we first need to point out what is wrong and identify the misplaced values which are causing our problems. We also need to explore concrete steps which we could take to move in the direction of greater responsibility.

At the international level, the redemption of debt is a good example: it is quite wrong that poor countries go on paying more in interest than they receive in aid so that they simply get poorer and poorer. In the same way, we need to look at the whole question of the arms trade: the five permanent members of the Security Council provide 80% of the world's arms. Sadly, we tend to become accustomed to the way our world is: the Millennium provides us with an opportunity to take stock of the ways in which we need to change it.

Ms Humera Khan: On the basis of my own experience, and that of others I know, I do believe that there is a need within society for defined norms and standards. In a country where Christianity remains the majority religious faith I have an expectation that the Church will offer sound moral leadership and direction and establish some clear boundaries for ethical behaviour. I am disappointed that the Church is reluctant to meet this need.

I have lived the whole of my life in inner London within a multi-cultural and multi-faith society in which many people experience confusion over their identities. Adolescence is very difficult to handle in the kind of society we have. There is a need to establish clear parameters and guidelines for children as they grow and develop so that they at least have a starting point from which to build their framework of values. Sadly, there is a spiritual vacuum within our society. In my view religious leaders have failed to meet this challenge. It is not enough simply to toss the problem back to families and to schools. Young people need to be helped on their journey in making sense of the reality which they experience in their daily lives. Those who seek secular counselling in an effort to deal with their confusion of spirituality are made to feel worse by being told that God is a figment of their imagination.

My own organisation is engaged in work at a local level, trying to help and support those who are in difficulties and need to be strengthened from within. All faiths point to the need for our inner, or spiritual, and outer lives to be in harmony with each other. I hope that we shall find clearer leadership from the church and other religious leaders in our society in encouraging this.

Dr Manazir Ahsan: I found the presentations we have heard today very interesting and useful. The presentation by the Chief Rabbi was very much in line with a Muslim understanding of the agenda for our society and I welcome and appreciate the way he has expressed it. Most often it is not realised that Western society is not only based on the Jewish and Christian traditions alone but also on the Muslim tradition and together they form the three Abrahamic traditions. Muslims are not newcomers to Europe; they lived in and ruled over the Iberian peninsula (modern-day Spain and Portugal) for more than seven centuries before coming to Eastern Europe and the Balkans, during the period of Ottoman rule. They brought a magnificent civilization and a superior culture to Europe and gained numerous converts not only in Spain, Sicily, and Southern Italy, but in the whole of the Balkans area.

These three faiths share many values and cultural traditions and I do not see any difficulty in establishing common values between them. Nor do I think that there is a problem in doing so with other faith traditions, as all of them have elements which are held in common. The work of the SCAA Forum is very valuable and we should all give it the strong support which it deserves.

At present, Western civilisation is passing through a severe crisis, with problems deriving from the breakdown of the family giving rise to problems at home and in the wider society. As the Chief Rabbi said, we need to devote our energies and resources to tackling these problems in our homes, in our schools and in our community institutions. We cannot do so effectively in isolation from one another if we are to find peace and happiness in our society.

Our schools need to reflect the values which we want to uphold in our wider society and we need to provide good examples to our children. It is right that schools should give children a values-oriented education based on those shared values which have been articulated, such as honesty, care for one another and the pursuit of truth, which the majority of us have in common, whether we belong to a particular faith community or not.

The media has a most important role to play. Too often it projects unhelpful images of our different faiths and Islam has been treated particularly unjustly. A better and positive image of Islam in Britain and other parts of Europe will create better opportunities for Muslims to foster better and friendly relations with people of different faiths. A negative and distorted image is harmful for community relations and meaningful inter-faith dialogue and discussion at a local, national and international level. The Muslim community needs to discuss this with the media and to encourage them to give a more accurate picture of Islam.

Mr Om Parkash Sharma: I agree with a great deal of what has been said by other speakers. I would like to offer from the Hindu tradition some of the teaching which Lord Krishna gave to Arjuna as set out in "The Bhagavad Gita". He said that people should have these qualities: "no violence in thought, word or deed; truthfulness and generosity in speech; an absence of anger, even under provocation; renunciation and restraint in action; composure of mind; abstention from malicious gossip; compassion towards all creatures; an absence of attachment to the object of our senses; mildness; a sense of shame when transgressing these standards; abstention from frivolous pursuits; forbearance; fortitude; external purity; bearing enmity to none; and an absence of self esteem." These are the marks of those who have been born with divine gifts. With these we can make a peaceful world. And in another Hindu text it says: "With righteousness in the heart comes purity of character; with purity of character comes beauty in life; with beauty in life comes harmony in the family; with harmony in the family comes equilibrium in the State; and this brings peace to the world."

Within the Hindu tradition it has always been important for students to acquire a pattern of values which will help them lead the good life and show them the path through which the noblest qualities of body, mind and soul can be developed. It is this kind of approach, rather than the lack of discipline and strict standards of conduct that is exhibited at present, that we need to be upholding in our education system.

Dr Helen Haste: Today has been very illuminating. I have been reflecting from a psychologist's perspective on what has been said. Many people have talked about giving precepts, or rules for living, to children. We have heard an expression of the "golden rule" from Judaism and some of the precepts of the Buddhist and Hindu traditions. These provide rules by which we might live. But, as Professor Parekh asked, a major question is how do we *motivate* people to live moral lives? How do we engage and energise people? Giving people rules to live by is fine if they are ready to accept them, but how do we get the population of a country energised to pursue the moral goals that we all want to achieve?

We know that the best way to get people involved in an enterprise is to make them believe that they can effect change as a result. The Festival of Light, mentioned by Bishop Gavin Reid, and CND are two examples of very different movements which won support by persuading people that they could make an impact through supporting them. In times of religious revival we see people of all ages who want to offer themselves in service to a god. How do we get children to want to make their own moral impact on the world?

The National Curriculum Council's document on citizenship which came out a few years ago was a masterpiece of compromise. To please everyone the suggested curriculum was filled with conventional ideas about involvement in the community including, for example, helping elderly people. At roughly the same time, the BBC published a markedly subversive document "The Blue Peter Green Book". The children's television programme, *Blue Peter*, has always had items about collecting bottle tops and helping people from the Third World. This "Green Book" offered, in effect, a curriculum for citizenship through engagement with environmental concerns. It was aimed at 8 to 10 year olds and sold over 150,000 copies. It motivated 8 year olds to write to their MP's about issues of pollution and to join organisations dedicated to improving the environment. Someone complained about it in the House of Lords, and was quite right to do so because it was indeed a subversive document! I contrast the blandness of the NCC's material on citizenship (which was in its way quite commendable) with the suggestions in the Blue Peter Green Book for more practical action and engagement in the political process.

If we want to get children engaged in moral action we must not just give them rules, but also a sense of *how they can make an impact* and make society better in practical ways.

Mr Lionel Benjamin: I speak from both a psychological and a Buddhist viewpoint. If we are to live up to high ethical values this can only be done as a result of training. This is often difficult and we resist undertaking it. I was brought up in the Christian faith and, looking back on what I learned through it, I see the Ten Commandments as a training manual to get a small band safely through a hostile country to the promised land: so you should not fight with your neighbour or the band will break up. The Ten Commandments were a way of binding the Jewish people of that time together. The Buddha would only give ethical guidelines when something had gone wrong, and needed to be put right within the community. So rather than giving generalised commandments he taught those around him how to behave better.

We need training for many purposes. In the Army people are trained to kill. We also train people in the skills of business and we train for sport, but we do not pay enough attention to training in the skills of the mind. All of us have trained for sport at school or elsewhere. This is always hard at first until the body gets used to it. But what about training in spiritual skills? If children have not seen, heard and practised these skills then we cannot expect them to behave well. When I was growing up my mother told me and showed me what to do and not do so that I knew what I should do and had the choice of doing it.

We have such inequality in the distribution of wealth within our society that some people can actually afford to destroy things for pleasure and to throw away items that are still in good working order. We have a society that makes things and break things at speed. Lord Rees Mogg said that in the future the rich will go on "making and breaking" while the poor will have to repair things and use them again. If we are to survive, we need to train for the future.

Mr Francis Baden-Powell: As Chairman of the Gresham College I am most grateful for the invitation to join you at this seminar.

Four hundred years ago when Sir Thomas Gresham established Gresham College, which was initially based elsewhere, his intention was to bring to people the "new learning" of the Renaissance to replace the "old learning" derived from religion. So it is appropriate today to be reflecting here about the communication of ideas, which has always been the role of Gresham College.

I am very involved with a number of schools of which I am a governor. I am struck by the way in which the main priorities of these schools relate to academic success. This again comes back to the question of the values in our society at large. We live in an atmosphere which values success and in which less thought is given to those who are less successful. In my view we need to focus on other objectives than just academic success, for example on self worth and self fulfilment and I try to encourage a debate on the need for this in the schools with which I am involved.

In this country we are suffering a crisis of self confidence. We are coming face to face with the recognition that over the last 100 years we have moved from being a "first league" country to one much lower down the scale. Yet the opportunities this creates are enormous and I hope that we will grasp the opportunity which the Millennium gives us to think about how we want our society to develop in the future.

I would like to give one example of the way in which we can encourage an involvement on the part of children and young people in the issues of the day. I am involved with a theatre company which focuses on homelessness, called Cardboard Citizens. Using homeless actors it puts on plays about homelessness in places where the homeless meet or in schools. Members of the audience can challenge at any point what the character is doing and then go forward and take over the playing of the part. I was recently at a performance at a school in the East End of a play about the descent of a girl into prostitution as a result of her rejection by her family and the lack of support she received at her school and then in the wider community. In the play her stepfather throws her out and she runs away. Youngsters went up to take over the part of this girl (and all of the audience were boys!) and the actors *ad libbed* around the way the audience wanted the story to develop. Within the space of quarter of an hour a number of different scenarios were played out.

This kind of dramatic presentation helps the young people to think deeply about the morality of the decisions which have to be taken as the story unfolds. It is important for schools to have sufficient time within their curriculum to explore moral issues and also to make available to them examples of the methodology of tackling these issues in ways which give them meaning for young people. The sowing of the seeds of moral awareness is a very important task for our schools.

Ms Melanie Phillips: When Bishop Gavin Reid referred to the media's concern with values in reaction to the Dunblane massacre and to Mrs Lawrence's initiative he suggested that this was possibly only a transitory phenomenon. I do agree that the media are not actually getting to grips effectively with the issues involved. There is a risk that an initiative like Mrs Lawrence's will just be used as a kind of media artefact to boost a newspaper's circulation and that it will be dropped as soon as the commercial possibilities of it are seen to be exhausted.

Why is media attention to these issues so fickle? Partly it is because the media are in the business of promoting the very same values that have brought about the present state of our society: a concentration on cheap thrills, instant gratification, sensationalism, voyeurism, mixing up the public and the private, and the divorce of sexuality from marriage and procreation. This is very much the agenda of the popular media, designed to sell its products on the basis that human nature has been debased so that people will, for example, buy *The Sun*, folding it inside their copy of the *Catholic Herald* or whatever! So to a large extent in the values debate the media are being invited to host a critical debate on precisely those values which they themselves are busy purveying. This is a very significant obstacle to their playing an effective role in this debate.

What struck me about the coverage of Dunblane and of Mrs Lawrence's initiative was a note of astonishment on the part of many media commentators that the debate sparked by these incidents had apparently come out of nowhere. But this was a profoundly wrong perception. People are desperately worried about their children and other people's children, children who are out of control, problems of parental authority , the state of our schools, and the level of crime. There is a great deal of anxiety around and it only needs a few sparks to bring all these concerns to the surface. Generally speaking, in the absence of sensational events like Dunblane and the murder of Philip Lawrence the media do not pick up these issues. Why? I think it is because by and large the media are divorced from real people and their real life concerns.

Bishop Gavin Reid alluded to the fact that the media treat the Churches very badly. I do not think you can overestimate the almost visceral hostility of much of the media culture to the Churches and to religion in general. That is a very worrying phenomenon. Why is the media so hostile to "religious" values and to values in general? There are various reasons for this. The media think that the Church is boring and out of touch and that most people are secular and do not go to church. The media do not like other centres of authority that tell people how to behave. For one thing, they may try to interfere with the media's own agenda! But I would also like to suggest a more controversial reason. The media are not just hostile to the Church because they disapprove of it but because they are in the business of replacing the Church!

The media see themselves as our secular priests and the mediators of the prevailing culture. Why is this so? It is because the Church has abdicated its position of moral leadership within society and this has created a vacuum in terms of values into which the media have leapt. They have sensed an opportunity here to take greater power for themselves. Journalists are now much more powerful than they were even twenty years ago. This is because they are filling a vacuum in both political and religious leadership. The institutions to which we should be looking for moral, spiritual and cultural leadership have abdicated their position.

Bishop Gavin Reid expressed his gratitude to the Chief Rabbi for being so "up front" about religion. He related the experience so far of the discussions on the Millennium in which the Church has been apologetic and timid in putting forward its own religious point of view. It has prevaricated about those root problems of our society which preoccupy most people. The Church of England has, for example, been exceptionally equivocal on marriage and the family. Its instinctive reaction over the Millennium has been that it does not want to give offence to others. It is concerned about the risk of being seen as excluding rather than including people as a result of promoting its own message. It has put the desire not to offend or exclude at the top of its priority list. It is this same desire always to achieve consensus which is the basic trap into which the SCAA Forum exercise is at risk of falling.

On media involvement in a national debate on values, by all means approach the media moguls in the hope that they will decide to help to promote this. There is still a certain amount of civic responsibility on their part and that of editors and senior journalists. But it is no use appealing to them to take the initiative on moral regeneration as long as the Churches and other institutions continue to fail to exercise effective moral leadership within society. If the Churches provide this leadership it will put the media's role into a proper perspective. At the moment they are enjoying the power they can exercise in filling the vacuum that has been left for them.

Rt Revd Charles Henderson: In our discussions today we may not have found all the answers and indeed we may not have found the right questions. But we have started a process of meeting and interchange at a personal level and of being able to speak openly and honestly with each other. No doubt everyone here will disagree with at least some aspect of what others have said. But at least we have listened. My understanding of the relationship between the media and the Churches is not the same as Melanie Phillips has just described. But, nevertheless, I listened with interest to what she has said and she has made me think more deeply about it.

There is always a danger of misunderstanding in our exchange of views because we do not always speak the same language. I myself come from Ireland from an Irish cultural and educational background but I have since experienced living in multi-cultural Britain. I do believe that it is realistic to suppose that we can find common values; and a common approach to living in harmony with one another. We can find parameters which we all respect and which would enable us to live in peace. We can do this if we seek to know one another better. There is an adage: "Know yourself". Knowing yourself, and valuing yourself enables you to know others and to value them equally as yourself. If you can begin to exchange views and concerns with other people on equal terms and be prepared to listen, then, even though there can be misunderstandings, the heart will eventually overcome these.

One of the problems of our present age is the strength of individualism as a philosophy: pursuing one's own interest regardless of others. This is a deeply damaging philosophy of life. I am convinced that as individuals we must accept a responsibility which starts with the freedom of the individual, but this freedom does not mean license to do as one wishes. Rather, freedom starts with the need to respect the freedom of others. We need to uphold freedom and the responsibility which goes with it rather than license coupled with an individualism which excludes a proper concern for others. I am sure that this offers a basis on which we can find common values and a common way of life.

Mr Nicholas Coote: The Chief Rabbi spoke about the importance of the role of the family, the school and the community and, by implication, of these in contrast to the State. The recent document produced by the Roman Catholic Bishops of England and Wales, *The Common Good*, calls for "the remoralisation of the public sphere", without which families, schools and the community will all find themselves in difficulty. This document reflects the teaching in recent Papal documents, which have used the phrase "the structures of sin". The Pope is pointing to the fact that our society is caught up in certain structures which make it difficult for individuals to reach moral decisions and to carry these out within the family and the community. We need to remoralise the political enterprise and to reclaim it from professional politicians.

Mr Brian Pearce: We need to draw our afternoon's discussion to a close. The current debate suggests that we can reach agreement on shared values in terms at least of the "core" values we hold. Inevitably more difficulty arises when we try to apply "core" values to particular situations where there may be a clash of values which seem to pull us in different directions. But it is important for us not to lose sight of the significance of our ability to establish a degree of understanding on common "core" values. We need then to go on to discuss with one another in more detail the implications of the values we hold for particular spheres of life and how they apply in varying circumstances. Questions of process and of how we can create a framework within which this continuing debate can take place fruitfully are also of great importance. I hope that the space and time we have provided today has been a contribution to that process. It seems to me unlikely that the debate about morality, about values and about virtues will come to a premature conclusion, removing the possibility of any "Great Debate" linked to the Millennium! The debate will surely go on.

*   *   *

Close of Seminar

Mr Pearce then invited *Mr Om Parkash Sharma*, the Co-Chair of the Network, to conclude the seminar. After reciting a Hindu prayer, Mr Sharma said that he hoped that participants felt, as he did, that the day had been a most valuable opportunity to hear about a number of current initiatives in the field of values, both in education and in our wider society and to exchange reflections on that debate and how it could best be carried forward. He expressed particular thanks to the main speakers, the Chief Rabbi Dr Jonathan Sacks, Dr Nicholas Tate, Ms Monica Taylor, Professor Bhikhu Parekh and Bishop Gavin Reid, whose presentations had been both stimulating and enlightening. He also thanked all the seminar participants for being present and for the contributions they had made to the formal and informal discussions in the course of it. He thanked Mr Brian Pearce, Dr Harriet Crabtree and Mrs Harsha Shah of the Network office for their work in preparing the day's seminar and repeated his thanks to Gresham College for the opportunity to hold it at Barnard's Inn Hall.

Annex A
Statement on Values by the National Forum for Values in Education and the Community of the School Curriculum and Assessment Authority

[Ahead of the seminar, by way of background, participants received copies of the consultative document issued by the School Curriculum and Assessment Authority in November 1996 on the work of its National Forum for Values in Education and the Community. The document included a statement of values which had emerged from its deliberations. Following a further meeting of the Forum in January 1997 and other consultations, some adjustments to the text of the values statement were made and a preamble setting it in context was added to it. It is the text of this revised document which is reproduced below.]

The Preamble to the Statement of Values

The National Forum for Values in Education and the Community was set up by the School Curriculum and Assessment Authority to:

1. discover whether there are any values upon which there is common agreement within society;
2. decide how schools might be supported in the important task of contributing to pupils' spiritual, moral, social and cultural development.

The Forum identified a number of values on which members believed society would agree. Extensive consultation showed there to be overwhelming agreement on these values.

The second part of the remit was met by the recommendation that SCAA produce guidance for schools on the promotion of pupils' spiritual, moral, social and cultural development. This guidance, it was recommended, should be structured around the contexts of value, build upon current good practice, encourage rigour and a whole school approach to work in this area and be supported by booklets of case studies, a directory of resources, a glossary of the terms commonly used in this area and guidelines for community service. It was also recommended that the guidance include suggestions on how the school might involve the local community to work in this area. SCAA was also asked to use the statement of values nationally to instil confidence, trigger debate and elicit support for schools in the vital task of promoting pupils' spiritual, moral and social development. This work is currently being planned.

It is important to note the following points:

- The remit of the Forum was to decide whether there are any values that *are* commonly agreed upon across society, not whether there are any values that *should* be agreed upon across society. The only authority claimed for these values, accordingly, is the authority of consensus.

- These values are not exhaustive. They do not, for example, include religious beliefs, principles or teachings, though these are often the source from which commonly-held values derive. The statement neither implies nor entails that these are the *only* values that should be taught in schools. There is no suggestion, in particular, that schools should confine themselves to these values.

- Agreement on the values outlined below is compatible with disagreement on their sources. Many believe that God is the ultimate source of value, and that we are accountable to God for our actions; others that values have their source only in human nature, and that we are accountable only to our consciences. The statement of values is consistent with these and other views on the sources of value.

- Agreement on the values is also compatible with different interpretations and applications of these values. It is for schools to decide, reflecting the range of views in the wider community, how these values should be interpreted and applied. So, for example, the principle 'we support the institution of marriage' may legitimately be interpreted as giving rise to positive promotion of marriage* as an ideal, of the responsibilities of parenthood, and of the duty of children to respect their parents.

- The ordering of the values does not imply any priority or necessary preference. The ordering reflects the belief of many that values in the context of the self must precede the development of the other values.

- These values are so fundamental that they may appear unexceptional. Their demanding nature is however demonstrated both by our collective failure consistently to live up to them, and the moral challenge which acting on them in practice entails.

Schools and teachers can have confidence that there is general agreement in society upon these values. They can therefore expect the support and encouragement of society if they base their teaching and the school ethos on these values.

---

*In British law, marriage is defined as 'the voluntary union for life of one man and one woman to the exclusion of all others'.

THE STATEMENT OF VALUES
THE SELF

We value ourselves as unique human beings capable of spiritual, moral, intellectual and physical growth and development.

On the basis of these values, we should:
- develop an understanding of our own characters, strengths and weaknesses;
- develop self-respect and self-discipline;
- clarify the meaning and purpose in our lives and decide, on the basis of this, how we believe that our lives should be lived;
- make responsible use of our talents, rights and opportunities;
- strive, throughout life, for knowledge, wisdom and understanding;
- take responsibility, within our capabilities, for our own lives.

RELATIONSHIPS

We value others for themselves, not only for what they have or what they can do for us. We value relationships as fundamental to the development and fulfilment of ourselves and others, and to the good of the community.

On the basis of these values, we should:
- respect others, including children;
- care for others and exercise goodwill in our dealings with them;
- show others they are valued;
- earn loyalty, trust and confidence;
- work co-operatively with others;
- respect the privacy and property of others;
- resolve disputes peacefully.

SOCIETY

We value truth, freedom, justice, human rights, the rule of law and collective effort for the common good. In particular, we value families as sources of love and support for all their members, and as the basis of a society in which people care for others.

On the basis of these values, we should:
- understand and carry out our responsibilities as citizens;
- refuse to support values or actions that may be harmful to individuals or communities;
- support families in raising children and caring for dependants;
- support the institution of marriage;
- recognise that the love and commitment required for a secure and happy childhood can also be found in families of different kinds;

- help people to know about the law and legal processes;
- respect the rule of law and encourage others to do so;
- respect religious and cultural diversity;
- promote opportunities for all;
- support those who cannot, by themselves, sustain a dignified life-style;
- promote participation in the democratic process by all sectors of the community;
- contribute to, as well as benefit fairly from, economic and cultural resources;
- make truth, integrity, honesty and goodwill priorities in public and private life.

THE ENVIRONMENT

We value the environment, both natural and shaped by humanity, as the basis of life and a source of wonder and inspiration.

On the basis of these values, we should:
- accept our responsibility to maintain a sustainable environment for future generations;
- understand the place of human beings within nature;
- understand our responsibilities for other species;
- ensure that development can be justified;
- preserve balance and diversity in nature wherever possible;
- preserve areas of beauty and interest for future generations;
- repair, wherever possible, habitats damaged by human development and other means.

Annex B
List of Participants

Dr Manazir AHSAN
Director, The Islamic Foundation, Leicester; Vice Chair of The Inter Faith Network

Dr Hamid AL-MAJED
Director, The Islamic Cultural Centre, Regent's Park, London

Mr Francis BADEN-POWELL
Chair, Gresham College Council

Mr Lionel BENJAMIN
The Buddhist Society

Revd Marcus BRAYBROOKE
Chair, World Congress of Faiths; International Interfaith Centre, Oxford

Ms Maggie BUTCHER
Gresham College

Mr Nicholas COOTE
Assistant General Secretary, Roman Catholic Bishops' Conference for England and Wales

Dr Harriet CRABTREE
Deputy Director, The Inter Faith Network

Ms Eileen FRANCIS
VECTOR (Values Education Consultancy Training, Organisational Research); Vice-Chair, Values Education Council

Ms Zerbanoo GIFFORD
Director of the Asha Foundation

Mrs Ivy GUTRIDGE
Woverhampton Inter Faith Group; Vice-Chair, The Inter Faith Network

Ms Helen HASTE
School of Social Studies, University of Bath; Chair, MOSAIC (Moral and Social Action Interdisciplinary Colloquium)

Rt Revd Charles HENDERSON
Auxiliary Bishop in the Archdiocese of Southwark; Chair, Committee of Other Faiths of the Roman Catholic Bishops' Conference for England and Wales

Mr Ted HUDDLESTON
The Citizenship Foundation

Rabbi Dr Julian JACOBS
Adviser to the Chief Rabbi on inter faith matters

Ms Humera KHAN
Al-Nisa Society

Revd Stephen LYNAS
Archbishops' Officer on the Millennium

Dr Peggy MORGAN
Westminster College, Oxford; Shap Working Party on World Religions in Education

Mrs Gwen PALMER
Chair, Steering Group on Joint Review of Collective Worship; former Chair, Religious Education Council

Professor Bhikhu PAREKH
Professor of Political Theory, University of Hull; former Deputy Chair, Commission for Racial Equality

Mr Brian PEARCE
Director, The Inter Faith Network

Ms Melanie PHILLIPS
The Observer

Mrs Rosalind PRESTON OBE
Vice-Chair, The Inter Faith Network

Dr Andreas PRINDL
Provost, Gresham College

Dr N.K. PRINJA
Education Adviser, Vishwa Hindu Parishad (UK)

Dr Andrew PURKIS
Adviser to the Archbishop of Canterbury on Public Affairs

Rt Revd Gavin REID
Anglican Bishop of Maidstone; Chairman of the Archbishops' Millennium Advisory Group; Deputy Moderator of the Churches Together in England Working Group on the Millennium

Ms Darshan SACHDEV
Senior Research Officer, Barnardos

Rabbi Dr Jonathan SACKS
Chief Rabbi of the United Hebrew Congregations of the Commonwealth

Mrs Harsha SHAH
Administrative Assistant, The Inter Faith Network

Mr Om Parkash SHARMA
President, National Council of Hindu Temples; Co-Chair, The Inter Faith Network

Mr Indarjit SINGH OBE
Convenor, Network of Sikh Organisations (UK); Vice-Chair, The Inter Faith Network

Revd Io SMITH
Joint President, Council of Churches for Britain and Ireland

Rabbi Jacqueline TABICK
Associate Rabbi, West London Synagogue

Dr Nicholas TATE
Chief Executive, School Curriculum and Assessment Authority

Ms Monica TAYLOR
Chair, Values Education Council

Most Ven. Dr M VAJIRAGNANA
London Buddhist Vihara

Mr Stephen WHITTLE
Director, Broadcasting Standards Council